Through Struggle, Strength: My Journey from Paralysis to the UFC

Cole Escovedo

With Zac Robinson

Through the Cage Door: My Journey from Paralysis to the UFC

© 2014 by Cole Escovedo, Zac Robinson

ISBN-13: 978-1500721527

Cover photo courtesy of Jeff Sherwood, www.sherdog.com

All rights are reserved. No part of this book may be reproduced in any manner without the written permission from the author except for brief passages used in a review in newspapers, magazines, or web sites.

Zbooks LLC

Prologue

I couldn't feel my legs. They had turned into two useless attachments that just sat there, unmoving. My stomach was swollen to the point that it looked like I had swallowed a basketball. I was pumped full of drugs, but the pain was unbearable. My head throbbed and my body burned as if it was on fire from the inside out. Later, I learned that I was allergic to morphine. It was one of the drugs that coursed through my veins in an effort to ease my pain. It was having the opposite effect.

The gurney I was lying on was being wheeled through Valley Medical Center, past the gangbangers sitting in the metal chairs in the lobby and the low-income families desperately seeking care for whatever ailment they were suffering from. The hospital lights hurt my eyes. I squinted against their harshness. My world was out of focus and rocked with uncertainty.

I was sure that even after the surgery I would be paralyzed for life. My career as a professional cage fighter would be over. To say I was scared would be an understatement. I was petrified. I'd worked so hard for everything I had earned.

Now it was all gone.

I was wheeled into a room with even brighter lights. The pain in my head screamed. Then my mom, Laura, was there. She is as strong as they come and my number one supporter. Through the fog and pain I looked at her. She tried to mask her concern, but even through my drug-induced haze I could see she was racked with worry.

My neurosurgeon arrived.

"Okay Cole, I want to give you one more chance to consider your options. We can have the surgery, but once again I want you to be fully aware of the dangers. If even the tiniest mistake is made you will definitely be paralyzed."

This information rolled around in my brain. I had heard it before, but now I was literally minutes away from going through with the surgery. "And my other option, Doc?"

"Take the medications. They may or may not work and you will most likely remain paralyzed or have to use a walker."

I'd had heart surgery prior to my fight career, and I'd had numerous surgeries due to fighting, so I was no stranger to the risks. "I still want the surgery," I said.

My mom couldn't take it. "I've got to have a cigarette," she squeezed my arm and left the room in a hurry.

They were about to begin prepping me when a strange thing happened. I got a little bit of feeling in my legs. It was a shock to me because I'd been getting worse and worse, not better.

My younger brother, Cody, had just arrived. I didn't know it at the time, but he saw Mom outside. She was smoking her cigarette and banging her head into a wrought iron fence.

It had been a horrible month of not knowing what was wrong with my back and struggling desperately to find out while I wasted away. Understandably, she was distraught.

"I can't do this anymore, Cody. I just can't," my mom told my brother when she saw him outside the hospital. "You've got to go talk to Cole."

Cody came back to the room and I told him about my legs. He looked as confused as me with this recent turn. I told the doctors as well and again they asked if I wanted to go through with the surgery. "Does me having a little bit of feeling right now change anything?"

The answer I got, "Basically, no."

The surgery was risky, but in my mind it was my best chance.

Cody had left the room earlier, now he came back with Mom. Obviously, he had told her about me having some feeling in my legs. "Don't do the surgery!" She clung to the hope that I could recover without it.

"No, I've got to have the surgery," I replied.

"You're not even in your right mind right now, Cole."

It was true that my brain was flooded with drugs, but I felt clear enough to make the decision. "I have to do it Mom. It's the best option."

She wasn't so sure about that, but she finally gave in. "Okay, but I can't do this. Your brother is staying with you."

It was time. The doctor went over everything one last time and the anesthesiologist prepared to administer the drug that would turn my lights out.

This was it. My world was about to go dark. I would wake up with renewed hope or the crushing pain of a lifetime in a wheelchair.

I thought about my life: the early years in the trailer, karate classes, the night I learned my dad had been arrested, the terrible visits to prison, the days of drug dealing, the police academy, my beautiful daughter and what I went through to get her, all these memories, good and bad, marched through my head as if I was trying to hold onto them. They had all helped forge my attitude of never quit and always pay the necessary price to receive victory. I was paying a very odd and heavy price right now. In a way going through with the surgery was a last ditch effort to not quit on hope.

Then, as the Anesthesiologist stuck the needle into my vein my life as a pro fighter dumped into my thoughts: the exhilaration of the first victory, beating Philip Perez and claiming the WEC belt despite the fear of being shot, Poppies Martinez and the insanity surrounding it, Urijah Faber and the street fight beforehand, Jens Pulver's left hook, Antonio Banuelos...the drugs started to take hold and my vision blurred. My eyes drooped.

Would those memories be all I had? Would I ever get to make new ones? Would I ever take another step on my own again?

My eyes closed completely. I was out.

Chapter 1

I guess it's safe to say that I was a fighter from the start. Or as my mom says, "I was supposed to be here."

She has a few reasons for making that statement. There was the time she was pregnant with me and trying to break her mustang. The horse threw her straight over its head. She hit the ground and rolled. I must've felt the impact, but I definitely don't remember. "Damn, that looked like the rodeo," my dad, Larry, said. "Do it again!"

Luckily my mom chose not to give it a second go.

Then there was the time she was on the back of my dad's Panhead Harley. They were doing about 65 miles per hour when he hit a threepenny nail. He lost the front end and pushed my mom off before he went down with the bike. My mom landed in a bush and both of them were banged up, but she didn't lose me.

And then there was the bar fight. My mom has told this story many times before, and I know it well. Right before she knew she was pregnant with me she was in a Hell's Angel bar with my dad. They were in a motorcycle club and weren't afraid to mix it up if needed. When she tells the story I can almost see it coming out of her mind and being painted back into real life.

Willie Nelson's "On the Road Again" gave way to Waylon Jennings' "Mama Don't Let your Babies Grow up to be Cowboys." The songs came from an old-time juke box and sliced through a cloud of smoke to reach the ears of bar patrons that came with slicked back long hair, tattoo-covered arms, and motorcycle leather. And somewhere on each member of the bar was a knife or gun, or both.

Larry and Laura, the soon-to-be parents of one Cole Escovedo, sat at the bar sipping on cold beers alongside their friends and other regulars. As Waylon sang about mamas needing their kids to be doctors and lawyers and such, a non-regular sidled up to the bar to the left of Larry. He was a big white guy with scraggly hair and a look on his face that said he wasn't a happy drunk. Larry leaned over to Laura. "Move down. I want to get away from this guy."

They slid over, but kept watching him in the mirror that was mounted behind the bar. He ordered a Coors. As soon as the bartender slid the bottle his way, he stood up, gripped the neck and swung it hard. Larry ducked, but it was a split second too late. The bottle crashed into the back of his head. Beer and blood sprayed everywhere.

Larry was about five foot seven and a hundred and fifty pounds. The guy who just tried to plow the bottle through his brain had almost a hundred pounds on him. Larry fell out of the stool, but remained on his feet. Before he could recover though, his attacker picked up a barstool and slammed it over Larry's head. He went to a knee, but with blood running like streams down his dark

Apache face and dripping off his nose and high cheek bones, he came up swinging. His turquoise and silver rings that encircled every finger, his "just in case brass knuckles," found their mark.

Laura, and by extension me, jumped onto the guy's back. She clawed at his eyes and punched him in the back of the head. She didn't notice that when Larry came up swinging he had pulled his knife from his right hip and started cutting.

The fists and blood were flying and it was a chaotic mess. My mom, who was unaware that Larry was stabbing the guy, kept clawing. He turned sideways and Larry's blade grazed my mom's stomach. Inches more and I probably wouldn't be here.

The man fell. Larry jumped on top and grabbed his hair. His blue shirt was soaked in blood and he brought the knife to his attacker's throat. In a minute the big hillbilly would be lying in his own growing pool of blood.

"You have to stop it. No more!" the bartender yelled.

Laura helped pull Larry away, and with a bandana covering the license plate and her steering while Larry slipped in and out of consciousness, they rode home.

After it was all said and done, Larry had stabbed the man 32 times. Amazingly, he lived. And luckily for an unborn me, I did as well.

Chapter 2

As my mom's belly grew, the police investigated the fight and stabbing. They were all over the bar, but nobody gave my mom and dad up. "It was two white guys...a white guy and a black girl...they had afros..." These were just some of the variety of descriptions the detectives got from those at the bar. After some pleading from the bar owner my mom called the detective.

"Hey, you've got to get off our asses man. Leave these people alone."

It was the correct conclusion, but it still surprised my mom when the detective said, "We've decided it was self-defense."

And that was it. They were off the hook.

I, on the other hand, wasn't off the hook when it came to joining this world. My mom was young, just 20 years old, and she didn't know much about having a baby. Her mom wasn't around. She was mentally ill and had been in and out of institutions for much of my mom's life. Then of course my mom ran with a motorcycle club so she didn't really have anybody to ask about what to expect when having a baby.

It was a scorching hot late August day in 1981 when my mom went to the hospital to have me. The hospital was packed and the contractions were getting closer and closer together. She had expected to get an epidural and then pop me out with no problem. And the nurse was about to come in the room to give her that epidural when all hell broke loose.

She was hooked up to the monitors and they started beeping and going crazy. A nurse hurried into the room and she was followed by another. They both wore professional, but very concerned looks.

"What the hell?" my mom said.

"It's the baby. He's flat lining."

My mom went into a complete panic. She'd had no drugs, not even an aspirin, and now they needed to get me into this world right away.

My dad started to freak out as well.

The doctor arrived. "The baby is dying," he quickly explained to Larry. "We have to get it now and it is very dangerous for your wife. If it comes down to it, do we save your wife or your child?"

Larry looked at my mom and back at the doctor. "Save her."

My mom wasn't really supposed to hear this conversation, but she did. "Hell no, Larry! You save my baby. You'd better go call my dad right now."

Larry wasn't sure what to do, and he hesitated.

"Dammit Larry, go call my dad, NOW," my mom yelled through painful gasps as she contracted again.

Calling my mom's dad wasn't exactly high on Larry's list. He was from the wrong side of Fresno and he in essence had taken my mom away from her family when she was just 14 years old. And they lived on the "right" side of town. My mom was nearly six feet tall and a blond-haired ballerina, but she fell for an Apache Indian with a pony tail down to his ass and a violent streak that reared its ugly head all too often. My mom had run away with him and fell into a crazy lifestyle of partying and drug dealing.

Now, as Larry left the room to make the call, her dad was on the verge of losing his grandson or his daughter and he wasn't even aware of it.

With no medication and the contractions intensifying, the doctor yelled at my mom to push me out. "Push, push, push! We have to get the baby out now or we'll lose him."

My mom did her best. Pain ripped through her and sweat rolled from her dampened hairline and trickled down her face. During the contractions and her monumental effort to push me into the world she'd managed to tear out the IV's. Blood dripped all over the hospital bed and floor.

This all happened in an ER room because a delivery room was unavailable. During the chaos, and while Larry was still gone, a delivery room became available. They rushed us into it.

My mom gave one more excruciating push. I was born with the cord wrapped tightly around my neck and I was an ugly blue color. My mom collapsed from exhaustion. The doctors and nurses went to work on me and then rushed me away to the ICU.

In the meantime, Larry returned to the room that now had an empty bed that looked like it was the scene of a Texas Chainsaw style massacre. He was sure one of us or even both of us was dead, and he went on a rampage.

I was in an incubator and my mom was in a recovery room. "Hey, did you hear about that crazy Indian?" the lady next to her asked.

"What?"

"Yeah, he's running up and down the hall screaming and jumping on nuns!" It was a Catholic hospital. "He was yelling, 'Where's my wife?'"

"Uh oh," my mom said.

Fortunately, it all worked out and no nuns were hurt during my hectic birth. However my dad would end up hurting other people in the not too distant future.

I spent two days in an incubator. For a while the doctors weren't sure I would pull through, but as I mentioned before, I was a fighter from the start.

The doctor said the way my birth went down was something like one in a million, but a few years later my little brother, Cody, was born almost the exact same way.

Chapter 3

About a week after my wild birth my mom brought me home. Our home was a tiny singlewide trailer on a couple of acres just outside of Fresno. The door squeaked loudly every time it was opened and you had to walk up a couple of weathered wooden steps to get to it. Once inside, it was clean and neat for the most part, but it was almost like living in a hallway.

We were in the trailer until I was five years old. There isn't much need to remember anything about my first home, but my mom does tell a story that was something of a prelude of things to come.

We all slept in the same room. My mom and Larry in a small bed and me right next to them. One night my mom woke up to the smell of gasoline. She rolled over and noticed Larry wasn't in bed. She checked on me and I was breathing softly, sound asleep.

There was a noise from the side of the trailer, something clanking against something else. My mom jumped out of bed and shuffled across the worn shag carpet to the front door. She swung it open and looked left and then right. She saw nothing, but heard another noise around the side of the trailer.

Larry's motorcycle was parked out front so she knew he hadn't gone anywhere. It must be him making the noise, she thought. My mom walked down the steps and circled around the side of the old gray trailer. The stench of gasoline made her face crinkle. She put her hand over her mouth with her thumb and finger pinching her nose.

Just before she turned the corner there was another loud clang. She picked up the pace.

She saw Larry next to the back porch. He stood facing the trailer and a red gas can was on its side next to his bare feet. He wore no shirt despite the chilly night and his hand was deep in his jean pocket.

"What the hell are you doing?" my mom said.

As my dad looked at her he pulled a blue Bic lighter from his pocket.

My mom took a couple steps toward him. "Larry!" she yelled. "What the hell are you doing?"

As she asked the question again, his intentions became very clear. He was about to light the trailer, with me inside, on fire.

This time, my mom got his attention. He looked at her with glazed eyes. "I guess, I guess I was sleepwalking or something." He looked down at the lighter and shoved it back in his pocket. Then he walked back inside.

The next morning they talked more about this bizarre incident. My mom was young and eventually accepted Larry's explanation. It wasn't until much later when she came to the realization that my dad had the symptoms of multiple personality disorder. When he was a young boy he had been horribly abused by his own father. This most likely triggered his disorder and created the monster, as he called his other violent and evil personality.

Growing up, I didn't have to deal with "the monster" really. I can thank my mom for this because she loved my dad and he felt safe with her. I think this kept his other personality at bay.

Other people weren't so lucky.

Not long after the near torching of our little trailer my mom and I were sitting inside watching TV on the couch. There was a banging at the door. My mom walked across the small living room and opened it. A couple cops stood on the wooden steps.

They were looking for Larry. "We have a warrant for his arrest," they said.

"What is going on?" my mom asked.

They went back and forth as my mom tried to find out what was going on and they kept asking where Larry was.

"I'm not telling you where he is."

My mom was insistent, but then they told her they had a warrant for her thanks to an outstanding ticket for parking the wrong way on a street. "We're going to take your baby and take you to jail," the taller cop who had been doing most of the talking said. "You're an accomplice to armed robbery."

There was no way in hell my mom wanted me to end up in the welfare system and now she was really confused about what was going on. "Okay, I'll give you Larry if you let me take Cole across the street to my girlfriend's house."

The cops agreed and my mom told them that my dad was at work. They held up their end and let my mom take me to the neighbors before arresting her.

She was in and out of jail because she didn't have any priors. They just used it as leverage to find Larry. Once she was released she called him. "You'd better get the fuck out of there because they're coming for you," she told him.

During the visit to jail my mom was able to piece it all together. A couple weeks earlier Larry and his friend Bob ran out of beer. They made a trip to the 7-Eleven at just a few minutes before two in the morning when beer sales had to stop in California. The clerk wouldn't sell it to them because it was so close to two. They briefly argued back and forth and then Larry had enough. He pulled his gun out and waved it to the clerk while informing him that they'd just go ahead and take the beer.

Larry never mentioned a word of this to my mom because it was "the monster" and not him. He just went about his business until the 7-Eleven clerk happened to drive by our trailer and noticed Larry's motorcycle out front. He called the cops and they showed up and arrested my mom even though she had no idea about the 7-Eleven robbery.

Finally, Larry made it home. My mom was pretty damn pissed and eventually talked him into turning himself in. He ended up spending three days in jail and my mom's dad had to put up his house for bond. Upon release, my dad had a crazy story.

He looked at Mom with wild eyes. "You're alive! Where's Cole?"

"He's at the babysitter's. Why?"

"While I was in they took me down to the basement and beat me with a rubber hose. They kept telling me I was a hit man for the Los Dorados and I was going to kill a sheriff. Then they said, 'Because of that, we're going to take out your wife and kid.' All the time I was in I was sure you two were dead."

Of course my mom flipped out and came to get me. She didn't know what the hell to believe, but spent quite a while looking over her shoulder and keeping me close by. Nothing ever happened after it and we managed to get my dad's sentence busted down to just a year of community service.

It wasn't until almost 20 years later when my mom found out that much of what they said was apparently true. It was reported to her that Larry was supposed to hit a sheriff, and the guy who told her this also said, "Fuck yeah he was going to do it. There's all kinds of shit he did that you didn't know about."

This isn't what my mom wanted to hear, but at least it was a long time after the fact, and I had grown up to be someone who could take care of himself just fine when the occasion called for it.

Chapter 4

I was almost three years old when Cody came along. When I was born with the cord around my neck the doctor had told my mom it was a one in a million birth. Amazingly, Cody was born the same way. When he came home my dad decided it was time for us to get out of the singlewide.

We moved out of the trailer to a place in Clovis and then on to a ranch house in Madera just outside of Fresno. It was two stories and its light blue paint blended with the sky. It was set a little bit off of the road and a gravel driveway with fence posts on either side led to front of the house. The front was actually hidden behind two big trees that provided much needed shade during hot summer days. The back of the house was complete with some outdoor wooden steps to the second floor and it looked out over our dirt yard that was enclosed by a wooden fence. It was quite a step up from the trailer.

The last few years had been relatively quiet and my parents were slowly working their way up. Nobody had gotten in trouble with the law for a while and my dad had started working nights as a welder and soon became a shop foreman. He wasn't always able to hang out with me, but when he did I didn't see the monster. Sometimes I'd help him work on his motorcycle, sometimes we'd go fishing and I almost always enjoyed it. Other times he'd use a bungee cord and strap me down on the bike with him and we'd go cruising. It was awesome, but my mom wasn't too big of a fan of it.

My mom was hitting the books in college and just finishing up her second degree. A few years earlier her best friend, who was a hooker, told her she was smart and she should go to college. She took the advice to heart and had now started making a name for herself working in law offices. In effect, my parents had left the motorcycle gang and drug life behind.

One evening when I was six years old and Cody was just a toddler my mom came home with some tapes from Blockbuster. We'd just gotten a nice new TV and she popped a tape in the VCR. "I'm sure you're going to like this one, Cole."

She was right. Over the next two hours I watched in awe as Mr. Miyagi taught Daniel LaRusso the art of Karate. I was just a little kid, but I felt like my life had changed. As soon as Daniel pulled off the Crane kick and everybody celebrated, I hit rewind to watch it again.

Since we moved into the house I was in a new all white school. My dad is a full-blooded Apache and I was taught many of the old ways when I was young. My black hair was long and I wore it tied up in a pony tail that stretched down my back. The traditional ways of my Native American heritage helped instill the warrior spirit that I have today, but back when I was a six year old it also got me a lot of problems.

It didn't help that I was a string bean with coke bottle thick glasses and silver front teeth. I was bullied constantly. The day before I watched The

Karate Kid I had been at the water fountain at the school. I was minding my own business getting a drink after coming in from playing. Two kids walked by and one of them made "Indian sounds" with his mouth. The other laughed and said, "I'm gonna cut your pony tail off you little four-eyed girl."

My body tensed with a mix of hurt and anger. I wanted to turn around and beat the hell out of both the boys making fun of me, but I just didn't have it in me. Instead, I finished my drink and tried to ignore them. I was a little guy with just a little bit of confidence. I was an easy target for the others.

Now though, while sitting on our couch and watching The Karate Kid on our new TV for the second time in a row, I felt like maybe I did have it in me. I could be like Daniel and give Johnny and the Cobra Kai gym what they had coming.

I found my mom and dad upstairs in their room. "I want to start taking Karate!" I said.

They weren't so sure about it, but told me they'd consider it.

The next day at school, the same two boys started picking on me again. Something inside of me twisted and I clenched my fists and clamped my silver teeth down against my bottom row of teeth.

"That's it!"

I launched myself at the boy. He was bigger than me. I didn't care. I swung at him and he grabbed my shoulders and pushed and pulled trying to avoid getting hit. My glasses flew off so I didn't see the principal coming.

He lifted me up and threw me over his shoulder like I was a rag doll. The boys looked on in disbelief, and then the second one broke into a smile. The first was breathing hard and his face was red, but he had a smug grin on his face as well.

My mom came to the school and I told her what happened.

The principal entered the room. I'm sure he was prepared to punish me. Instead, my mom went honey badger on him.

"We have a problem here," he started to say.

"Damn right we have a problem," my mom interjected. "My son is getting bullied and picked on and he finally defends himself and you pick him up like that!"

She lifted herself out of her seat as she spoke. The principal leaned back with a surprised look on his face. He stumbled through an explanation and my mom continued to let him have it. Finally, we left. I was out of school for the rest of the day.

In the car on the ride home my mom looked at me. "I know you've had trouble at school with other kids. I hate that they pick on you and it makes me want to kick their parents' asses."

"If I can take Karate I'll be able to take care of myself." I said.

"I don't necessarily want you beating other kids up, but it might give the confidence you need to stand up for yourself and stop the bullying."

"So I can take Karate?" I asked excitedly.

"Yeah, we'll sign you up soon."

"Yes!" I pumped my fist as my mom pulled into our driveway. As soon as I got out I threw an awkward crane kick.

At school the next day I didn't know what to expect from my enemies. They didn't bully me, and I knew that if they started bullying me later on they'd get what they deserved soon enough.

At the time I never could have guessed that The Karate Kid and a scuffle at school would create a turn in my life that would help shape it many years into the future.

Chapter 5

I stood at attention in the center of the dojo listening to our head instructor, Tom. He was barking out a count in Japanese while doing blocks: Ichi, Ni, San, Shi, Go, Roku... The gym was decorated with Japanese-themed paintings and swords. Keeping with the Japanese theme, I was standing on a foam Tatami mat. The mats that covered the floor were designed to absorb some of the landing when thrown on them. They definitely didn't absorb all of the landing. Many nights I had gone home bruised and battered after being thrown on my back repeatedly.

A persistent smell of sweat, karate uniforms, and old equipment hung in the air. I didn't mind it. Sensei Tom finished demonstrating the drill. He'd expect us to get it right from the start. He was something of a drill instructor in the gym. He barked orders at us and had a heavy-handed style of teaching.

I learned very quickly that I had a natural affinity for martial arts. I loved learning the kicks and punches and Katas. It had taken just a few classes for me to feel more confident as well, and the bullying at school wasn't nearly as persistent.

However, I went to karate to help get away from the bullying, and yet in a strange way I was still getting bullied thanks to my Sensei's teaching style.

He actually reminded me of Sensei John Kreese from the Cobra Kai School in The Karate Kid.

He taught us and he taught us well, but he didn't pull any punches. His philosophy could be summed up like this, if you're going to learn to throw a sidekick you're going to learn to take a sidekick, and that's exactly what happened one night.

I had been practicing with a partner. Each of us took turns throwing ten sidekicks and then holding the bag. I was getting better and better and it felt like with each kick I was gaining more power. My partner held the bag firmly, but I moved him a couple feet every time I drilled it. I felt like I was Daniel LaRusso himself.

Sensei Tom came over and watched a couple kicks. "Turn your back foot for more power. Use your hips, Cole."

I did so and my kick was even stronger.

"I said turn your foot," Sensei Tom said in his aggressive tone. "Here," he handed me the bag, "like this."

He then stepped back and blasted the bag. I felt his foot drive all the way into my ribs and I tumbled over onto my butt. It hurt like hell, but I was determined not to show it. "See, that's what happens when you turn your foot and get your hips into it."

I stood up. "Yes Sensei," was all I could say.

This was fairly normal for my early experience with karate. It wasn't that Tom was a mean guy. He just taught in a very aggressive way. He would even go all out when he sparred with the kids. This rubbed a lot of parents the wrong way and they took their kids out of the class.

It was rough, but for me it was great because it helped to bring out more of my warrior spirit and taught me how to handle myself. Now nobody was making fun of me at school. Or I should say nobody made fun of me more than once. Not that I beat them up, but I definitely wasn't an easy target.

During those early karate days I met Matt Smith and I ended up working with him throughout the start of my MMA career. When he opened his own school years later, I followed him, but that was still in the distant future and I didn't know it at the time, but I'd have to deal with a whole lot in my life first.

Chapter 6

Things had smoothed out at school, and at the dojo I was dealing okay with the overly rough stuff from Sensei Tom and taking in all the positive stuff he taught me. I was starting to grow some and carried myself differently. I did still have my thick glasses and long pony tail though.

One Saturday morning we were doing a demonstration at the gym. The parents sat in bleachers on the side and we went through Katas, threw fancy kicks, and did one-step sparring. We finished with actual sparring and I felt like I was on it. Everything was clicking and every now and then I'd glance at my mom and dad. I could tell they were proud.

It wasn't until years later when my mom told me of the exchange she had with another mother. The other mom said, "That little girl is such a good fighter."

"That little girl is a boy, and he is a good fighter isn't he," my mom replied.

"I think you're wrong. That's a little girl."

"Nope," my mom laughed, "I know he's a boy because he's my son."

I guess I still had some growing to do, but I was doing my best to bring out my warrior spirit and it was starting to show, at least in some ways.

Not long after the dojo demonstration I was in the back of our house playing with my neighbors, the Delsid brothers. They decided they wanted to run away toward their grandpa's house. He lived a long ways away through a bunch of orange orchards and on the other side of I-99.

I knew it wasn't a good idea to run away, but as their friend I was worried they'd get lost or hurt so I decided to come along with them.

We rode our bikes through the fields for what seemed like hours. Sometimes we stopped and ate oranges and drank some water, but I noticed the shadows were growing and we were in no man's land. "We should go back," I said. "Our parents are going to be worried and it will be dark soon."

"I think we're almost there," the oldest Delsid said. "Let's keep riding. The highway isn't too far ahead."

I gave in, and we rode on. I couldn't have known that while we were gone my mom had come home and started looking for me. After a while she called 911 and it launched a search for us. We had ridden so far that they weren't searching in the right area and the assumption was that we had been kidnapped. The police even asked my mom for my dental records.

The sun sank into the Pacific and we had almost reached the highway. We passed a farmer on his tractor and he gave us a strange look. I didn't think anything of it at the time, but three kids all under ten years old riding in the dark through fields had to seem odd.

About 20 minutes later we were at the highway when a police car raced up to us with the lights flashing. The car skidded to a stop and the cop jumped out. "Is one of you Cole Escovedo?"

I got scared. We were in serious trouble for riding so far, I was sure of it. Finally, I spoke, "Yes sir, I'm Cole."

A relieved look crossed his face. "Thank God you boys are alright."

He radioed it in and soon we were riding back home in the police car with our bikes loaded in another one.

When we pulled up to my house, my mom ran toward the car. She hugged me tight. "I'm so glad you're okay, Cole."

"I'm fine Mom," I felt embarrassed.

She pulled away and held me at arm's length. There were tears in her eyes. "What in the hell!"

I looked down. "The Delsids wanted to run away and I wanted to make sure they were safe."

She lifted up my chin. "Oh Cole, I'm glad you wanted to look out for your friends, but don't ever do that again. I can't begin to tell you how horrible it is for a mom to think she lost her child."

"I won't, Mom," I said.

It was at this time that I really started to realize how much I meant to my mom. She had always been on my side and stuck up for me, but now I knew just how important I was to her.

Looking back, it was a crazy thing for us kids to do, but this trip, along with the school bullying and karate helped to begin to formulate my approach to life. I was slowly growing into being someone who would fight for what he needed to fight for and do anything for his friends.

Chapter 7

It's important to do everything you can for your friends, but sometimes that can come back to bite you. I learned this lesson not long after the trip through the orange orchards.

It was a blazing hot summer afternoon and my mom was at work. She had been working a lot as a paralegal and was on the verge of being accepted to law school. It seemed like she was doing a great job and her efforts would become very important soon.

Despite an addiction to Reds and being an alcoholic, my dad had been working hard as well in a really dangerous part of Fresno. Sometimes he didn't come home at all at night and I knew my mom worried about him from time to time, but I also knew he could take care of himself. Cody and I didn't see him too much because he kept odd hours.

We had gotten an above-ground swimming pool and my brother and I and another kid from the neighborhood, Art, were all swimming. It was a great way to have fun and beat the heat even though it was Art who was with us. He was that kid in the neighborhood that nobody else really wanted to play with. Sometimes he was dirty and he had a hard time getting along with others. I remembered those times a few years ago when I was the outcast and I got picked on, now I was a greenbelt in karate and had plenty of friends so I tried my best to be nice to him.

We swam and splashed and were having a great time when Art decided to dive in from the side. He knew the pool wasn't deep enough for diving, and yet he did it anyway. He came up out of the water and I said, "You're not supposed to dive. It's dangerous."

"Come on, Cole. I'm fine."

He then climbed up on the side to do it again. "Don't dive, you ass," Cody said.

Art shrugged his shoulders, "Whatever, *Ass*" he laughed and dove.

When he came out of the water his face was ashen and he was holding his neck.

"I told you not to dive," Cody said.

"I can't move my neck."

Cody and I thought he was screwing around, but it soon became obvious that he wasn't. He slowly climbed the ladder. We helped him down the other side and then helped him put his shirt on. Then Art stiffly walked home while trying not to move his neck.

The following day my mom got a phone call. Art's family was suing us because he had broken his neck in our pool. "That's complete bullshit," I said when my mom relayed the information.

I was right, but we had to get a lawyer and it was a good thing my mom knew so much about the legal system. They really came after us and Art showed up with their attorney in a big halo. Apparently he broke his neck, but it wasn't like his spinal cord was snapped. I looked at Art and I could tell he didn't really want to be going through all this. Deep down he knew he screwed up.

"The pool was dirty and there was no indication that it was unsafe to dive," their attorney said.

This was so untrue, and that day we went straight home and shot a video of the water and the signs that showed that it was dangerous to dive and no diving was allowed.

We finally went in front of a judge and he was showed the video. "It looks to me like the water is clear and I can see signs posted. I don't understand why you would dive head first," he said.

"Well it wasn't that way the day before," Art's mom said.

"You expect me to believe that they drained the pool and refilled it in 24 hours and took video in broad daylight and put signs up that look slightly worn?"

"Yes, that's what happened," she replied.

I glanced across the table at their lawyer and he had an exasperated look on his face. He, just like the judge, recognized that they were grasping.

"Let's assume what you say is correct," the judge turned to Art in his neck brace, "did anybody tell you not to dive?"

I could see the wheels spinning as Art tried to figure out how best to answer. I remembered exactly what my little brother had said, and then Cody, who was sitting on my left, spoke up.

"I told him, 'don't dive, you ass.'

I swear I could almost see the stone-faced judge's lips curl into a little smile.

That comment in effect ended the lawsuit. And it taught me that sometimes even people you are trying to help can turn on you.

Unfortunately for us, it would not even be close to the last time we'd have to deal with the courts.

Chapter 8

I wasn't sure what it was, but something had woken me. It was raining pretty hard and every so often there was a crash of thunder. Maybe that was it? It was the middle of the night on January 24, 1995, and the house was cold. I had a thick blanket pulled all the way up to my ears. I remained motionless with my eyes open, listening for whatever had brought me out of sleep.

There were four hard bangs from the front of our house and I heard footsteps in the hallway. Our old faithful Doberman, Apocalypse, let out a few deep barks as a warning. Adrenaline shot through me. I pushed the blanket away and swung my legs out of bed. My feet landed on the cool floor and I sat, listening. I was now 13 years old and a brown belt in karate. I was ready to defend my mom and brother if needed. There was another bang, and I heard a muffled voice. It was gruff. I thought it said, "Fresno police department, open up."

I stood and grabbed a t-shirt off the back of a chair. I pulled it on as I walked out of my room. I saw my mom just before she opened the front door. She was in a long t-shirt that read *Real Men Marry Lawyers.* Her blonde hair was pulled back. The look of concern on her face told me she had the same thoughts as me. It was never a good thing to have the police show up at your house in the middle of the night. This was about my dad, and my mom and I feared he was hurt or dead.

He worked late in the rough part of town and still ran with some really bad people. And even though he was good to me and Cody we knew the monster was there. If he was on Reds and full of liquor, which had been the case in the past, there was no telling what he could have gotten into. It had also been a long time since he hadn't come home once off work. Tonight had been different. He didn't show up and now the police were here.

I stopped and watched from a distance. She didn't know I was there. She stood in the opening and I heard the policemen talking to her. I could only make out a few words. "Arrested...serial...search..."

"Be quiet. My kids are sleeping," my mom said. "And there has to be some mistake."

Again the officer talked and I couldn't quite hear him.

"What for?" my mom said.

More muffled talking.

Finally, my mom stepped back and pushed the door open all the way. A policeman stepped inside. He kind of pointed toward her shirt. "Are you a lawyer?"

My mom didn't answer. She just glared at him. I turned and headed back to my room. On the way I saw Cody. He stood in the hallway with sleepy eyes and a worried look on his face.

"What's happening?"

"I'm not sure, but the police are here," I told him.

I ushered him into my room and we sat down on the bed.

A moment later my mom entered. She had the phone in her hand.

"Is something wrong with Dad," I tried to not let my voice become unsteady.

My mom rubbed her temple with her free hand and then leaned down close to us. "The police are here because they are saying your dad did a bad thing."

"What kind of bad thing?"

"Really bad," she said. "It's got to be BS though. Come down stairs with me to the couch."

We followed my mom as she dialed a phone number. The policeman I saw a moment ago still stood just inside the doorway. I noticed there were a handful of others outside. Later I learned that there were three agencies outside our house: the Fresno PD, the Madera PD, and the Fresno Sherriff's department. Whoever my mom had called answered as we sat down on the couch.

She walked toward the kitchen, but I could still hear her. She was calling the lawyer she worked with. "Larry has been arrested and the police want to search the house."

She listened for a few seconds.

"No, they don't have a warrant."

Again, she waited.

"One of them is already in the house. He's standing in the doorway."

More instructions came from the other end.

"Okay, I will."

She hung up the phone and turned back toward us. It was obvious that my mom was going through hell. Her eyes were red and puffy, but she didn't cry. Instead, she offered us a thin smile in an effort to reassure us.

"I have to talk to the police."

She was gone for at least ten minutes. I caught the first part of what she said. "You can't come in without a warrant."

The cop didn't like this one bit and they talked back and forth. Now I felt like I had the role of reassuring Cody. He was just ten years old and he'd been woken up on a perfectly normal January night to police wanting to enter our house and news that his dad had been arrested.

I tried my best to comfort him, but the truth was that I was in just as much shock as him. It seemed like in an instant my life had been ripped apart. I vaguely hoped that this could just be an ultra-realistic dream, but of course it was not. Instead of being asleep I was wide awake on the couch, and for the rest of the night we'd wait with the officer who was itching to bring his buddies in and destroy our home.

Chapter 9

As the night wore on it seemed like the cops multiplied. They were like vultures circling a wounded animal. They kept complaining about being outside in the storm. Their patrol cars were getting stuck in the mud in our pastures and their irritation was rising to a rolling boil.

Another officer came to the door. He spoke to the one inside. "The dog is threatening us. We're going to have to put it down if it isn't kept under control."

"Like hell you are," my mom interjected.

She went outside and got Apocalypse chained up so they wouldn't have an excuse to hurt him.

At some point in the night the silence was broken by the ringing of our phone. It was on the end table by the couch and my mom picked it up. There was a little crack in her voice. "Larry, why? What's going on?"

She started walking toward the bedroom and the cop tried to follow her. She spun around and told him to stay where he was.

I gave the officer a go-to-hell look as well and followed my mom. I was close to her and I heard my dad let out a deep sigh full of regret. "Okay, I guess I'm a bad guy."

My throat was tight and I was struck with the thought that just maybe he'd never be coming home again. I was still unaware as to exactly what he had supposedly done, but it was obvious that it was really bad. It was also obvious that my mom didn't believe that he did it and an aura of resolve formed around her. I could see it in her eyes. She was determined.

I didn't know exactly what the police wanted to look for and it took a while before I really heard why they wanted in. I was just 13 years old and didn't have any concept of the adult world, so when I heard the words serial rape I couldn't comprehend them.

As the sun was just about to come up in the east an officer produced a search warrant for my mom. He handed it to her. "He's being charged with 35 felony counts."

I thought the cop looked familiar and then it hit me that he lived down the street. His wife used to cut our hair. It was so surreal. It was as if a jagged line had been cut into our lives and people we knew in one capacity were now here in a completely different capacity.

My mom didn't respond. She just sat down and looked at the warrant. I had no clue even how to begin to respond. My dad was in jail. Police were now swarming our house. I felt like somebody had shaken our world until it turned sideways and scrambled everything. Nothing made any damn sense.

Cody had fallen asleep on the couch. Despite all the craziness around us, I had dozed briefly during the night. It was now morning time and if we didn't have cops all over our house we'd be getting ready for school.

My mom came into the living room. "Should I wake Cody up for school?" I asked.

She sat down and put her arm around me. "No, I think you two had better stay home today."

Normally this would be cause for celebration. Not now. Now, I actually wanted to get away. I just couldn't wrap my head around all that was happening. Sure, sometimes my dad would be happy one minute and then mad the next, but Cody and I were pretty wild and we just figured we did something wrong that we were unaware of. It never crossed our mind that our dad had severe problems and was capable of committing a terrible crime. Yeah, we knew he had some issues, but he treated us good and he was our dad.

One of the officers walked into the living room. He held a sawed off shotgun and another officer was right behind him with a handgun. "These your guns?" one of them said.

I was sure my mom would say no. We didn't own any guns. I looked at her and she glanced at me. "Yeah, they're ours. You can't take the .25."

The officer said something about being able to take it and started walking for the door. I didn't hear his words because I was too dumbstruck. As far as Cody or I knew we didn't own any guns.

The search went on for at least an hour. Finally, the police left and my mom came over to us. "Listen, I have to go get your uncle and find an attorney. I have to come up with a lot of money for bail. You guys are okay to stay here right?"

I nodded that we were fine. "How much money, Mom?"

She gave one of those smiles that were filled with pain. "A lot more than we have. I'll be back as soon as I can. Things might get tough around here, but we'll make it."

A moment later my mom raced out of our muddy driveway in her 300zx. It would turn out to be one of the last times she would drive it. She soon sold it to help pay for everything.

I looked out the front window and the kids all stood at the bus stop. It was right at the end of our driveway maybe fifty yards away. They had all gawked at our house minutes before when the police cars were parked in front of it. I felt confused and a little embarrassed even though I had done nothing wrong.

The bus pulled up and the kids, many of them my friends, piled on. They all looked back at the house and I could see the bus driver craning his neck to see if we were on our way. The bus sat there, idling. One of the kids said something to the driver. He gave a surprised look. All the kids were pressed up against the bus windows. They stared at my house and talked. I could only imagine what they were saying.

Finally, the bus made a hissing noise and pulled away. It was just Cody and me. The rain had stopped and our house was empty and silent.

Chapter 10

The calls started coming in later that day. Everybody wanted to know what was going on. It was terrible because we couldn't or didn't want to tell them much. The chance of bail had gone away. My mom instantly started selling our things to get the best counsel possible. Her car went fast. Then it was the motorcycles and a host of other odds and ends.

My mom and dad had struggled to work their way up in life and now it had been wiped away. The day after my dad's arrest, Cody and I went back to school. It was pure hell. Everybody wanted to know what happened. I didn't really have any answers for them. Two of my best friends, John Mosely and Steve Laswell, were there for me during this time in a big way and they supported me no matter what.

News about why my dad was arrested got out and suddenly many of my friends weren't allowed to come into my house even though I had done nothing wrong. My brother and I were ostracized for something we didn't have any control over.

One day, I got on the bus to ride home and somebody had scribbled *baby fucker* on the back of the seat. I looked at those words and boiled with anger and hurt. John saw the words as well. "Don't even let that get to you," he said.

I tried to shake it off.

Not long after the bus incident I learned that a handful of kids had decided to beat the hell out of me. They caught up to me on my street and I figured I was about to take a beating. Then John, who was already over six feet tall and a stud football player, stepped in, "You assholes need to leave Cole alone. He didn't do anything wrong."

They didn't see it that way. Things heated up in a hurry and I was ready to fight. John stepped in once again. "That's it, I'm getting my gun."

This threat kind of put things in perspective for everybody and John and I headed back to my house unscathed.

My mom was absolutely convinced that there was no way my dad was guilty. She launched her own investigation in an attempt to put doubt in the district attorney's mind. She'd talked to people and gone to places that might provide alibis for my dad. She took photos and scribbled notes on a yellow legal pad, filling up one page after another.

This, accompanied with her job at the law office and her visits to the jail to see my dad, meant she was working 16 to 18 hour days. I tried my best to continue to be a good kid. I'd make soup for her and wait up until she got home. I think many days it was just about the only food she'd eat because she was so busy and focused on exonerating my dad.

Despite my efforts, I felt the anger and pain growing inside of me. Cody and I had gone from having a stable family life with friends in the community to basically being orphans with our dad in jail and our mom working desperately to get him out.

It soon became a real possibility that we would be moving from our ranch house in Madera to a much smaller place in Clovis. It also became a real possibility that I would slip into a whole lot of trouble before this thing was all over.

Chapter 11

They called my mom "The Pit bull." She knew more about the case than anyone, so it hurt but didn't come as a shock when she learned that the prosecution was trying to exclude her because she was a witness. The unorthodox workaround for the defense was to simply appoint her to the case. This allowed my mom to be there from start to finish.

One night she sat at the kitchen table with papers and books spread out all over it. Cody and I sat at the table as well. She looked at us with determination. "I'm going to get your dad home."

This was not long after she was appointed. Years later, I learned it wasn't too long after this statement when my mom started realizing that it was very likely that Larry would not be coming home because he was probably guilty.

As the case wore on I continued to slip into a more destructive lifestyle. I still went to karate and earned my black belt, but I had lost a little bit of interest. I'd started hanging out with some different kids as well. They weren't as into sports, or at least martial arts, as me. They liked to party, and soon I started dipping my toes in that water as well.

My mom had hired one of the leading forensic psychiatrists at the time who had worked some very high profile cases, including the infamous Hillside Strangler case. He'd spent hours with my dad and later I learned that he thought it was very likely that he was on the verge of becoming a serial killer.

When my mom talked with my dad about this she said, "Were you thinking of killing me Larry?"

"Yeah, I was," he said with a melancholy tone.

"Why didn't you?"

"Because I love you and the boys."

My mom knew that his upbringing was filled with horror stories, but the extent of these horrors was becoming clearer as she fought for Larry's freedom. He'd draw terrible pictures of his life as a child, things one would have a hard time even imagining, and then he'd draw pictures of his life at our house. All over the drawing he'd write, *I love you, I'm safe.*

My dad spent his childhood being beaten and physically assaulted by the man who was supposed to care for him the most, his dad. He suffered for years and that second part of him, the monster, was born. Sometimes people would ask my mom how she could stay with him and defend him. "I married him for better or worse," she'd say. "Was he a good man? Probably not. Was he made that way because of his circumstances? Absolutely! So I don't condone the horrible things he did, but I'm with him. I want to help him."

One day not long after my mom found out about all the stuff that my dad went through as a kid we were driving through a parking lot when she saw Larry's dad. My mom reached under her car seat and withdrew a nine millimeter pistol. "Mom, you can't do that!" I said in a frantic voice.

For a moment it looked as if it didn't register. I had visions of her throwing open the car door and unloading the clip into my dad's dad. The look in her eyes was full of hatred and revenge. In essence it was this man who had destroyed our lives.

"Mom, don't do this!" I reached over and grabbed her arm.

It seemed like her eyes cleared. The reality of the consequences of killing him hit home and she knew that Cody and I would be parentless if she did it. She calmly slipped the gun back under the seat.

Because of my mom's unique situation with the case she actually knew who many of the witnesses were. And because of her past with a certain element of dangerous people she was presented with a plan to kill the witnesses.

"No, they didn't do anything wrong. Leave them alone," she said.

And later on, she was presented with another idea to help Larry escape when he was being transported from the jail to the courthouse. With her role to assist counsel she was privy to information that probably could have made an escape attempt very possible, but again she decided against it.

"Your dad would have ended up getting killed alone in Mexico and I wasn't going to force my kids into a life on the run," she told me many years later.

As it was, the case went to trial more than a year after my dad's arrest. The courtroom was somber, and as the verdict was about to come down a unique sense of tension sat over it. My father was being charged on 35 felony counts. I remembered how my mom had said she would bring my dad home, but as we got closer to the trial it seemed her resolve had shrunk. The more she learned the more she began to realize that he was guilty on at least some of these counts.

I watched the words tumble out of the judge's mouth. My dad was found guilty on 13 of the counts. His sentence was 68 years to life.

I felt numb. I felt like I needed to get away and either go beat the hell out of somebody or party my ass off. My hurt had been replaced with anger. My innocence had been destroyed by reality. I was barely into my teen years and now I had a convicted felon for a father and no male role model. I was lost.

Chapter 12

The car smelled like tuna fish. We were on the 99 heading north toward Pelican Bay State Prison. A few minutes earlier we'd blown through Merced. Modesto was on the horizon. This would be the first time we had gone this far away on our own. My mom was nervous and she packed a lot of food, including tuna fish.

Cody and I weren't exactly nervous. We were more pissed. Things had been on a steady decline since the day our lives were turned upside down. We used to have both parents and we'd wake up in the morning to Mom making breakfast and sit down at night to dinner with the family. Now though, Mom was working ridiculous hours each week and doing everything she could to make up for the financial stress that had been placed on us, and of course my dad was sitting behind bars.

We were on our way to see him for the first of what would become many visits. The prison is way up north almost all the way to Oregon about 500 miles away from our home. The drive seemed to drag on and on and on. My mom became more worried because we had been on the road for hours and it seemed like we should be there. We got caught up in traffic outside of Sacramento and had taken a couple wrong turns. Now we were on the 101 and there were signs for a place called Big

Lagoon. Darkness had settled over us and my mom rubbed her eyes.

"How close are we?" I asked.

"I'm not sure, maybe an hour or so," she replied.

There was a small motel up ahead on the right. I pointed to it. "Maybe we should stay there?"

"I was thinking the same thing," my mom said.

Ten minutes later we were settling into a tiny room in the crappy motel. It reminded me of Bates Motel from the movie Psycho, except it wasn't as nice. The room had just one single bed complete with a lumpy mattress. Cody and I got into our sleeping bags on the floor and I laid there wondering if I'd wake up with roaches all around me. Then I heard a sound. I realized it was my mom. She was crying, and it kept up for a long time.

"You okay, Mom?" I finally said.

She breathed deep. "Yeah, I'm okay. This is just so bad."

I nodded my head in agreement even though she couldn't see me. "It'll be alright," I finally said.

I went to sleep minutes later to the sound of my mom's soft crying.

The next morning we woke up early and drove the rest of the way to the prison. I had been upset because I felt like for so long Cody and I had been punished for what my dad did. Now we were being forced to take time away from our lives to drive all the way up here to no-man's land to see him. I mean I wanted to see him. He was my dad, but at the same time nothing had been fair for a long time now.

We were on a narrow two-lane road that was flanked by trees on each side. We drove in silence because I think all of us were a little nervous. We came to a stop light and made a right turn. The prison stretched out before us. There was a small guard shack and signs warning us that we were entering prison property and it held violent criminals.

After going through a series of checkpoints and my mom filling out a bunch of paperwork, we found ourselves in a room with tables, kind of like the school cafeteria except it had guards posted at various spots along the wall. A few other families sat at tables. We chose one and sat down.

I had not seen my dad in a long time. My foot bounced up and down in an effort to release some of the tension.

Then I saw him. He was in a yellow jumpsuit and white shoes. He looked thinner than I remembered. He saw us and offered a faint smile. My mom stood and they hugged. It was the first time she had touched him since the day before the police showed up at our house in the middle of the night. All the other visits had had glass between them. He shook our hands and we sat down to talk.

It was such a surreal feeling to be sitting here across from my dad. He was now a convicted criminal, and yet I remembered all the times we went fishing or worked on his motorcycle or just hung out and watched football.

He told us a little bit about his life in prison and we told him about what was going on back in Madera. One problem for my dad was that he was mixed in with the Mexican gangs. "You're going to have to give them proof of my Indian heritage," he told my mom."

"I'll get some paperwork and a declaration from the tribe stating that you are Native American," my mom said.

Finally, it was time to go. My mom and dad hugged. I thought I heard him say, "Sorry, Laura," but I couldn't quite make it out. Then he turned and shook my hand and then Cody's. "Be strong," he said.

I nodded, but did not speak. I was afraid my voice would betray me. We walked away with the promise of returning soon. And we did make that horribly long drive many more times over the next couple years. I hated it every time. The city next to the prison was always gloomy and rainy and reminded me of something from a Stephen King novel. The people kept to themselves, walking around with a hunched over posture that wasn't inviting. We stayed in a cheap motel and the drive was physically and mentally exhausting. None of us felt happy each time we drove away from the prison.

On the flip side, it allowed us a lot of bonding time. We'd gone from a two-parent household where they relied on each other like a team, to one parent overnight. Now our mom was our only safety net, during those horrible drives we talked and began to trust her and rely on her more and more. That was the only positive thread from those trips and it was very important, but it came at a steep price because of where my dad was. How much of a price? I'll never really know, but I did know that my life had been changed forever.

Chapter 13

I held the roach clip up to my lips and inhaled deeply. The smoke filled my lungs and I leaned my head against the headrest. I held the smoke in for a moment and then exhaled while turning my head toward the car window.

I watched the smoke drift through the crack and then looked over at my books sitting on the passenger seat. I grabbed them and hauled myself out of the car. Sure, I was high, but at least I was at school. I hadn't been at school very much lately. It was a waste of my time and the teachers pretty much just pissed me off.

I made it through first period, but during second period my history teacher kept going on and on about how important it was to know about some damn battle during the civil war. I started to doze off and it didn't make her too happy. She made a comment and I shot back. She got flustered and threatened to kick me out. I didn't give her the chance. I got up and left.

This had been part of my routine for some time now. After my dad went away I started a serious downward spiral. For a while I continued to go to karate off and on. It was the only link holding me to my past.

I ran some track as well and really enjoyed it because it was a one-on-one competition, line up and go and see who can get there first. So often it came down to who could reach deep down and find that little bit extra.

I remember running the 400 once and I was neck and neck with another kid. With some twenty yards to go I thought, push harder and you'll win Cole. I gave everything I had and won by literally milliseconds. It was probably the first time I ever really experienced that "leave it all out there" mentality. I almost threw up afterward, but I loved it. I also ran in relays and did the long jump and high jump and loved competing in them.

Unfortunately, as I climbed back in my car during the middle of the morning and lit up another joint, those track days and karate days were long gone.

I knew what I was doing was wrong, but I just continued to go down the bad path. Looking back on it I now know I was kind of lost at the time because my main male role model, my dad, had been taken away. I was mad at him for it and I was mad at just about everything else as well.

My world just didn't make much sense anymore, and despite my desire to do good for my mom, I just made bad choices. I drove around for a while and then finally went back home. My mom was dealing with her own struggles because the bankruptcy lawyer she had been working for was a lazy jerk. He'd pushed her to do more and more and would often miss court dates. When he told her she would start answering the phones as well, she drew the line and told him she wouldn't do it. His response...he fired her.

She was in a battle with him and it was putting a lot of stress on her, especially with all the other challenges she had with raising Cody and me on her own. She came home at around seven in the evening and her eyes looked tired. She gave me a thin smile. "I've got some interesting news for you."

"What's that?" I asked.

"We're going to Chicago to be on the Jenny Jones show."

Chapter 14

We sat in the green room on an ugly couch about half an hour before the show. There was a tray of pastries sitting on a coffee table in front of us. "I still say this is dumb," I told my mom. "We shouldn't be going on national TV to talk about our problems."

I'd made my feelings well known since my mom told me about this. I wasn't too high on the idea at all. My mom had already explained her reasoning to me many times, but I was young and had a hard time accepting it. "Think about it," I continued. "We're letting everybody invade our privacy."

"There are thousands of people out there with the same sickness your dad has," my mom replied. "Nobody is aware of it. Nobody is doing anything to help them. They're all just walking around like time bombs waiting to go off and nobody seems to care."

We'd talked about this after my mom told me about the show and also on the plane. Now I completely understand my mom's reasoning, but as we sat in that green room I didn't want to be the one to have to expose my life in order to help others. But my mom was ready to do just that. She figured that if we shed light on the issue it might give others the information they need to help a loved one before it was too late.

The first segment of the show started. It was a kid who was angry at his dad for being a member of the KKK. The dad was dressed in his full KKK outfit and the crowd was absolutely berating him. We quickly realized that the show was not like they had told us. They told us it would give us the opportunity to discuss our lives with a person suffering from multiple personality disorder. Instead it was more like Jerry Springer and they had titled the show, I hate my dad.

"This is not what they brought us out here for at all," my mom said.

"What do you want us to do?" I asked.

"Let's just see if we can get out there and get what we want out of it. We'll see if we can spit out what we want to spit out and then get off the stage before they can turn it into a circus."

Finally, it was our turn. They called my mom out and I watched as she did a really good job talking about multiple personality disorder.

Then it was my turn. They called me to the stage and I was immediately bombarded with questions from the audience and they kept belittling me. One guy stood up and yelled, "How can you hate your dad? What's wrong with you?"

"What are you talking about?" I replied.

Then they turned on my mom. "How can you support a guy who did that?" one woman yelled. "You have kids. What is wrong with you?"

The whole point of it was to get my mom and me to argue and then for the audience to pick sides so it would degenerate into a yelling fest. That was exactly what was happening. There was the KKK guy on the other side of the stage and people yelling. It was a complete Jerry Springer debacle.

Once we realized this we decided to get the hell off the stage.

The Jenny Jones show was pissed at us for walking off and they threatened us. My mom shot back that we were brought out on false pretenses.

In the end, the episode didn't even air. We think the biggest reason for this was that a black guy jumped on stage and got into an all-out fight with the KKK guy. I didn't even care. It gave us a free trip to Chicago, and besides, I was ready to get back home to continue my descent.

Chapter 15

Showing up to school high, ditching class to hang with my friends, telling teachers they were flat out wrong, and then proving it...I did it all. I had just given up on school and couldn't imagine myself graduating. This attitude made me feel like there was no real purpose for being there, but the real problem and what led to my expulsion was the fights.

At Sierra, if you weren't white or Indian, you were pretty much neutral, but I was half white and half Indian. The problem with this was that the whites and Indians didn't get along with each other and neither group accepted me because I was half and half.

I'd been having some serious problems with the Indian kids from the reservation. They'd all take their turn insulting me and throwing stuff at me. I tried real hard to keep from getting into fights with them, but fights happened. I had a string of them with the Indians and it seemed each one became more brutal.

I was still wiry and athletic despite my recent dip into drugs and booze. I had my karate background and I was starting to get into jiu jitsu. One day, a few kids from the rez were calling me names in the hallway and I fucking lost it. I turned on them and let loose. I dropped one of them and then kicked him in his ribs. Another one rammed me into the lockers and we both let our hands fly.

It was broken up pretty quickly, but the damage was done. I had a split lip and a swollen eye. All three of them had cuts and bruises and the one I kicked had a bruised rib. This led to another suspension, and it finally got the school officials off their asses.

The Indians really started threatening me, and my mom demanded that something be done before I returned to school. She even let it slip that she'd be more than willing to handle if on her own if needed. Finally, a conference was called. I rode with my mom and noticed she had a shotgun in the truck. I looked at her questioningly. "You think you'll need that?"

"I know how these things can turn out."

We walked down the hallway to where the conference was being held. There was a sheriff just outside the conference door. He had a serious look on his face and his gun on his hip. He nodded to us as we entered the room and my mom gave me a *see I told you,* look.

The conference room was huge and in the center of it was a wooden table that looked like it was designed for an executive's board room. All my teachers were there as well as the school principal and a couple other people I didn't know. I had assumed that some of the kids from the rez would be there as well, but they weren't. I thought that maybe the sheriff was there because the school thought that the Indians would try to make good on their threats with me coming back to the school.

The principal gestured for us to have a seat in two open chairs. We pulled them out and plopped down. I could tell my mom was boiling inside. She looked around the table at all my teachers. "So you all came for the hanging, huh?"

The principal, a short lady with beady eyes and curly dark hair, said, "That's not what this is."

But it quickly became apparent that it was indeed a bitch fest about me. I guess I kind of deserved it because I had not been the best of students by a long stretch, but at the same time I was the one who was being attacked and having to fight. Why weren't the Indians getting into trouble?

One teacher told me I was lazy. Another told me I would amount to nothing if I didn't change my ways. Another told me that she couldn't continue to have me in class if I kept behaving the way I was. And finally, another told me that I'd end up in jail one day.

This last one got my mom irate. "That's about enough. You're not here to help Cole at all." She pushed her chair away from the table. "Come on, Cole, let's go."

I stood, and we headed for the door. The principal, who was seated at the head of the table closest to the door, jumped up and blocked the exit.

"Excuse me. I'm not one of your students," my mom said. "Get the fuck out of my way."

The lady looked up at my mom and made the smart choice by moving to the side. My mom threw the door open.

"If you pass through that door, he'll be expelled," the principal said.

My mom spun around and looked directly at me. "Do you really want to stay and be taught by these people?

"Mom –" I started, but she cut me off.

"No, we're expelled, and you're out."

We stormed through the door and the sheriff had an unhappy look on his face. We drove away from the school and that was it. I was done there, and in effect it helped end my problems with the Indians. Then my mom put me in continuation school. I didn't last long there either.

Chapter 16

I was basically a complete outcast when I went to continuation school. There were a lot of other outcasts like me, except most of them were idiots. The teachers were boring and controlling and didn't challenge us in the least. The hours stretched on and on as the teachers spit out useless information.

Their idea of homework was to give us a workbook and tell us we had a week to finish it. The only problem was that it took me about a day to get it done. This gave me a whole lot of down time and I basically screwed around with it.

It didn't take long for me to get really bored and purposelessness. I started acting out more and more and questioning the teachers like I'd done in regular high school. Of course they didn't like this and we went back and forth. After only a couple months I'd had enough. One day I sat in class reading a book because my homework was done. I looked around the room at the other kids. They were a bunch of scrubs going nowhere in life, and I realized that with each day I was more and more like them.

Right then and there I decided that I was done with continuation school. I went home that night and told my mom. She wasn't exactly thrilled, but she understood. I was only 16 years old and now I was completely out of high school.

"You have to graduate, Cole. I don't care if you aren't in school. You still have to get your diploma."

"How am I going to do that?" I asked.

"The California High School Proficiency Exam, it's a test that shows you have learned what they teach in school."

I wasn't too fired up about this idea. I'd much rather spend my days smoking weed and doing a little bit of jiu jitsu. I'd started it not too long before and it was loosely structured. I'd show up and roll whenever I felt like it. It was a lot different than karate and I really liked it. I'd even competed in a couple tournaments. My mom was adamant though. I had to take that damn exam.

I studied off and on for about a month, and then went to a big building in Fresno to take the test. My mom threatened that if I didn't pass it I would have to go back to school, so I was pretty motivated.

The test was hard, but I felt fairly good about it. A couple weeks later I got a letter in the mail. I had passed. I was now done with high school and had time to do whatever the hell I pleased, and that meant smoking and jiu jitsu.

I fell into a ridiculously lazy routine, and one day my brother and I were riding around town with our three friends. They were brothers and everybody knew they were deep into dealing. Of course we'd been smoking and had other drugs in the car when Joseph took a corner too fast and smashed up a lady's fence. The car sat there idling with fence posts smashed up across her yard.

"Oh shit," I said.

"We're screwed," my brother Cody added.

"It's good, don't worry about it," Joseph's brother, Haroon, said.

The lady came out of her house and she was pissed. Haroon calmly got out of the car and looked at the damage to the fence. "I'm going to call the police!" the woman yelled. "Look at my fence. What's wrong with you?"

Haroon gave her a smile and raised his palms in the air. "Hold on, hold on. Don't complicate things by calling the police. We really didn't mean to bust your fence."

"Well it's still busted!"

"I know, but how much do you think it would cost to fix it?"

The woman calmed down a bit and scratched her arm while she thought about it. "I guess maybe $300."

Haroon reached into his pocket and pulled out a wad of one hundred dollar bills. He peeled off five of them and handed them to the lady. "This should cover the fence and any trouble that we have caused."

The desire to call the police had left the woman, and we drove away without any more trouble. Cody and I looked at each other. I could tell he had the same idea as me. It was time for us to start making big money like our friends.

Chapter 17

It had been just over ten years since I'd first seen The Karate Kid. Now, I was sitting on my couch watching it again. My mom sat in the chair next to me. We'd been talking off and on about what my plans were. I knew she was worried about both me and Cody.

About the time Daniel was starting to learn karate from Mr. Miyagi, my beeper went off. I'd recently gotten a cell phone, but at the time the beeper still seemed a lot safer. Cody and I had been dealing drugs for a while now.

After the fence incident we talked to our friends about it. They made it sound painless and easy and we knew we needed to make some money to help around the house. "I've got to go meet somebody, Mom," I said.

"Be careful," she replied.

My mom and I never really talked about what Cody and I were doing, but I got the feeling that she knew. She is one of the toughest and smartest people I know, plus she came up with the motorcycle club and running with gangs.

"I'm always careful." I shot her a quick smile.

I headed out the door and thought about my mom. She'd been through absolute hell over the last few years, and me or Cody, or both of us, getting arrested would not help her one bit. She'd lost the lawsuit against the attorney, and basically got blackballed from the legal community in our area. She'd tried to get other jobs with attorneys, but it seemed that she was seen as something of a threat. She was also denied unemployment and struggled along to find ways to make money to put food on the table.

For a while she was even talking to Peter Bloch at Penthouse magazine. They were going to do a story on my dad and everything that my mom had been through. I wasn't so sure about it, and then I found out that she'd have to pose nude.

"Hell no, Mom! You can't do that."

We argued about it for a while, and this time she gave in and nixed the article. I didn't know this at the time, but she also found out that my dad's family wasn't real happy with her. She'd been telling the story and a family member called to give her a warning that there would be "serious consequences" if she didn't stop exposing so-called family secrets.

She'd lost her husband and found out that he'd both been through and had done terrible things. She'd fought for her job and what was right, only to lose. And now it looked like our house might get foreclosed on. Then there was the fact that she was a single parent of two teenage boys who were drug dealers. At least we were smart dealers. It sounds cliché, but the first rule is to never use from your own supply. We did our fair share of drugs, but we followed that rule and it kept us out of a whole lot of trouble.

Our ranch was falling apart and my mom had told us that we were on the verge of having to sell it. One of the reasons we'd made the jump to dealing was because of our old dog, Apocalypse. Not long before the fence incident he'd gotten really sick. He was almost 20 years old and had been a part of the family for a long time. We wanted to take him to the vet, but we just didn't have the money. For a few days we tried to comfort him. He whined off and on and we knew that he was really sick.

Finally, one night I decided that I had to put him down. I took my rifle out back and said my goodbyes. I looked into his sad old eyes and knew he was in a lot of pain. I was doing the right thing, but pulling the trigger was still one of the hardest things I'd ever done. I had to do it for my mom and for Apocalypse, but damn.

Now, as I climbed into my truck I glanced at our house. The paint was peeling and a few other things needed to be fixed up. In a way I felt sorry for all of us. We had been dealt a pretty shitty hand and none of us fully knew how to deal with it.

I pulled out of the driveway to meet Haroon. He was going to give me a few ounces of weed to sell. It wasn't much, and I got the feeling he wanted to tell me something else.

A few minutes later I pulled in at the side of the convenience store. Haroon backed in next to me. He searched the parking lot with his eyes before rolling down a window. He gave me a worried look. "Some shit's going down, Cole."

Chapter 18

We'd found out that the house was definitely being foreclosed on. My mom was real good about stretching it out though, so we were able to stay in it while we worked to get everything in order. That way, maybe we could come out of it with a little bit of profit. We'd done some work to fix up some odds and ends, but we desperately needed to paint the house.

My mom just didn't have the money to do it. I talked to Cody and he agreed that we should approach mom about paying for it. She was sitting at the kitchen table going over bills and other papers. "Hey Mom," Cody said, "Listen, Cole and I can come up with the money to paint the house."

She looked up at us. "And just how do you have the money?

"Don't worry about that, Mom. We just got the money," I said.

She nodded, and I knew that she knew exactly where the money was coming from, but none of us were willing to get into it.

"So you want to spend your money to get the house painted?"

"Yeah, we definitely want to do that," Cody said.

"We want to be here for you Mom like you've been for us," I added.

She agreed, and we were able to get the house painted.

Around this time, the shit that Haroon had talked about was starting to hit the fan. The brothers were under surveillance and it seemed that the police were closing in on them. Of course this caused a hell of a lot of stress for Cody and me. We'd become the go-to guys for drugs in our area and were pretty high up on the food chain.

We continued to deal, but now we were much more cautious. It had seemed like easy money, and for a while it had been. Now though, the risk of being arrested seemed to be growing. After a few weeks, Joseph was deported and his brothers were in hiding.

This caused us to reassess what we were doing, and Cody and I decided to kind of back away from the dealing. We definitely didn't want to end up in prison, but then Cody got busted for stealing beer and the clerk almost shot him. He did three days in juvie and I had a bad feeling in my stomach that there would be more jail time in our future if we didn't change.

Just the thought of prison made me think of our visits to Pelican Bay to see my dad. For a while we visited every couple of months, but those visits became less and less frequent as time went on. I was fine with that. I hated every single visit to that hell hole, and I definitely didn't want to end up in a place like it.

My mom was trying to move on with her life too. There was a guy at work named Steve. He was always asking her to dinner, and during Christmas time she told me he said to her that nobody should be alone at Christmas. "Let me take you to a show," he'd said.

Finally, my mom agreed, and Steve and she became better friends with each day. I wasn't so sure about him. We rubbed each other the wrong way from time to time. One day on the ranch our cat had kittens and I was holding one of them when Steve came over. I stood with him at the back of the car. He pulled on latex gloves and then popped open the trunk. I glanced inside and there was a rifle. He's going to shoot me, I thought. I stepped back and raised the kitten in front of me.

He looked at me funny and reached into the trunk and pulled out some tools. "I'm working on the car," he said with a smile.

I decided Steve wasn't too bad of a guy. After all, he wouldn't shoot a kitten and that has to say something.

We finally lost the ranch and my mom managed to get $20,000 out of it. We moved into a small townhouse in Clovis. It wasn't as bad as we thought. My mom had told me that she had visions of battling the cockroaches on the south side. Instead, our 900 foot two-story brick house was decent and cockroach free, and Steve had helped us out a lot through the process of moving.

Cody and I were going through a lot of changes, and I could tell it was getting to him. My mom worried that he was exhibiting some of the same signs as my father, and ended up staying home with him most of the time.

I'd been dealing and doing jiu jitsu for a good stretch, and my friend, Matt Smith, had opened up his own school. I'd been going there and getting more and more into it and had even started competing. I also met two brothers, Dan and Dave Camarillo. They were big into jiu jitsu and pushing me to keep at it.

I felt like I was being pulled toward the gym, and I guessed that was a good thing. At the time I never could have predicted where it would lead.

Chapter 19

My days consisted of sitting around and smoking some weed and then rolling on the mat. I mentioned Matt Smith. I'd known him since I was a kid. He broke away from our old school and I decided to follow him. It was there that I started to get into tournaments and they intermixed with my earlier drug dealing days.

Dave Camarillo came up to me one day and asked if I'd come to a tournament in Bakersfield. At the time I was just 15 years old and still bouncing in and out of school. It would be my first jiu jitsu tournament. I went home and told my mom about it.

"I'm good with you going. I trust you and think you're in good hands."

With that, I got a shot of adrenaline in my veins and it felt good. I wanted to compete.

We rolled to Bakersfield in a caravan with Dave's red SUV leading the way. Bakersfield isn't exactly a vacation spot, and as we drove through the town we passed rundown buildings and the houses were small and busted up. We were in a bad part of town, but I didn't give a shit. I was ready to get on the mat.

As we got closer to the gym I felt a knot of excitement in my stomach. I asked Dave and Matt questions looking for any last-minute instruction that might make a difference. During the moments leading up to the tournament I felt more alive than I had in a long time.

The tournament was held in an old gym. There were four mats crammed onto the concrete floor and maybe 200 enthusiastic people scattered about. It was finally my time to go. Matt gave me a few final instructions and then I stepped on the mat. The guy I was competing against looked to be about five years older than me and he seemed confident, but once we hit the mat I realized that I was every bit as good as him.

We rolled for a few minutes before I saw an opening for an armbar. I locked it in and felt his tap. A sense of accomplishment washed over me as the realization of my first tournament victory set in.

Sweat trickled off my face and I was roughed up a bit, but my hand was raised. Right after I stepped off the mat, Dave came up to me with a huge smile on his face. He was committed fully to helping me and treated me like a little brother.

He gave me a big hug. "That was awesome, Cole!"

This made my sense of accomplishment swell even more.

It was an amazing experience, and as we climbed into the cars for the drive back to Clovis I had one thought, I want to do this again.

Not long after my first taste of jiu jitsu competition, I was on the mat for a two-day event in Las Vegas. I was really just a kid and the energy and excitement of Las Vegas was amazing, and then I hit the mat. I finished my first opponent with a triangle. And then I finished the next guy with a triangle as well. And then another and another. I won via triangle for every single one of my matches.

At the time I couldn't have known that the triangle would become my signature MMA move.

Chapter 20

After that great Las Vegas weekend I started competing fairly regularly. I loved that I could get on the mat with my opponent and it was just me and him. It was all in my hands to win or lose and I thrived in that environment.

I started working harder because I loved the taste of victory and wanted more of it.

One day, Dave pulled me aside. "What do you think about coming up to Mountain View with me to train with Ralph Gracie?"

"I'm not sure," I replied. "Do you think I'm good enough for that?"

"Yeah, I do."

We talked some more about it and I went home after class. On the way I thought about how cool of an opportunity it would be. My mom was in the kitchen doing some paperwork. She stayed with Cody pretty much all the time now because he was really struggling. It wasn't long ago when we found my mom's horse, dead. At first we thought it was shot, but realized that our other horse had kicked it.

It had rained a bunch and was so muddy that we couldn't get the horse out. It laid there for weeks until the ground dried and we could take him away. It was terribly hard on all of us. My mom loved her horses and took good care of them. And it was especially hard on Cody. The horse had been his dad's and it was the one he rode all the time. When it died he kind of lost his last connection to our dad.

Cody had already been having a hard time, and this really made it worse. My mom gave up looking for a job and did odds and ends jobs where she could stay home.

She looked up from her paperwork and gave me a weary smile. "How was class?" she asked.

"It was good. Dave wants me to come live with him at Mountain View for a while and train with Ralph Gracie."

"Really?" my mom's eye brows rose up in a questioning way.

"Yeah, he says it would be good for me. Can I do it?"

My mom thought for a minute. I knew she fully trusted Dave, but the idea of letting me go off somewhere else to be on my own was something she had to think about. After a long moment a smile crept onto her face.

"I think it would be good for you as well."

With that, I made the move to Mountain View with Dave. After seeing my new living arrangements I wondered if I was crazy. We were above an industrial carpet cleaning business. The apartment had cement floors and no heat. It was always wet and cold and there was no TV. All we had were movies and training.

The gym was like a dog pit. It was survival of the fittest and ten times tougher than anything I'd ever done before. I trained so hard every day and met guys like the Diaz brothers who would become friends for life.

It was like a breeding ground for competition and camaraderie. Even though we beat the hell out of each other we knew we were doing it to get better.

One night I was sparring Mike. I can't remember his last name, but he was a member of the Ralph Gracie fight team. We were going back and forth when he dropped me.

I stood up and he gave me a moment to recover. "Are you ready?" he asked.

"Yeah, I'm good," I replied. But apparently I wasn't good, because I thought I had my hands up but they were down by my hips. It was weird because I could have sworn they were up.

Dave Camarillo was coaching us and he stepped in. "I think that's enough for tonight."

I didn't argue with him.

Chapter 21

Even though I was doing well at jiu jitsu and training hard at Ralph Gracie's I still felt like I was doing basically nothing with my life. I trained and smoked and sat around watching TV, nothing else. My friend, John, the one who had my back when my dad got arrested and sent to prison, had been talking about joining the police academy.

It sounded kind of interesting to me, but at the same time I couldn't really see myself as a cop. I'd been the guy the cops looked for, so it was hard to wrap my head around actually becoming one.

One day not long after John had talked to me about the academy I was driving around town with Cody. We were just dicking around, not doing anything worthwhile. I turned a corner and it felt like a cellphone on vibrate went off in my chest. I let out a weird sound and clutched my chest with both hands, taking them off the steering wheel in the process.

Cody quickly reached over and grabbed the wheel before we drifted into oncoming traffic. I let off the gas and he guided the car to the curb.

"What the hell, Cole? Are you alright?"

I rubbed my chest hard and it started feeling better.

"You're pale," he said.

I glanced into the rear view mirror and he was right. I continued to massage my chest for another moment and the feeling went away.

"I don't know what happened. It felt like my heart started vibrating."

"Oh shit. Should we go to the hospital?"

"No, it's good now. And don't tell mom either. She doesn't need to worry about this."

"Are you sure?"

I exhaled deeply and rolled my shoulders back against the seat to stretch out my chest a little. There was no buzzing feeling and I felt fine. "I'm sure. I'm good. Probably just heartburn or something."

I didn't tell him that I'd had this sensation a few times before.

We went about our day and got home a few hours later. I was settled on the couch watching a tape I'd picked up at Blockbuster of one of the first Ultimate Fighting Championships from a few years earlier. Since I'd been training so much in jiu jitsu with Ralph Gracie and the Camarillos I'd gotten into watching UFC. The sport had been getting bashed in the media over the last couple years and I didn't know if it would last because of it, but the old tapes were awesome.

Dan Severn was throwing the much smaller Anthony Macias all over the cage when my mom walked into the room. "What happened in the car?"

I looked up at her. "Nothing."

"Don't give me that shit Cole. Cody told me that your chest started hurting so bad that you let go of the steering wheel."

"It was just heartburn or something. I'm fine now."

"I'm taking you to the doctor tomorrow morning."

"I knew you'd react this way. That's why I told Cody not to tell you. I'm fine! And I've got jiu jitsu tomorrow."

"Not until after you see the doctor."

I knew there was no use in arguing with her. "Whatever," I said, and turned back to the TV just as Severn was finishing Macias with a rear naked choke.

The next morning I found myself in the doctor's office. A female doctor checked me out and did a couple tests. After getting the results she gave us the news I had expected, "There's nothing wrong with him," she said.

Chapter 22

"Dude, you're already good at everything needed to be a police officer," John said.

Once again, he was trying to convince me to go to the academy with him. The same UFC tape was playing, but he wasn't letting me watch it. "Seriously, you're athletic, you know how to handle a gun, and you're a good driver. You'd be a great cop."

I scratched the side of my neck in thought. I really had been considering it because like I said, I wasn't doing shit with my life and now I was 18 years old. I felt like I needed to find something that would give me some purpose. Jiu Jitsu was good, but despite training with Ralph and seeing Royce Gracie dominate the early UFCs, I couldn't see me making a living with it.

I looked at John. He'd always been a big guy and he had always been sincere. His barrel chest stretched at his t-shirt and I could tell that he truly thought this would be good for me. He was already set on going, whether I joined him or not.

"Come on Cole, It will be fun."

"I'm in," I finally said. "Let's do it."

"Hell yes!" John replied.

The following day we did the paperwork and turned everything in. The idea of becoming a cop was still surreal, but the more I thought about it the more I had decided I wanted to do it.

I had to schedule a physical to get cleared. I wasn't worried at all about it because just days earlier the doctor had said my heart was fine, and I was in damn good shape from all the jiu jitsu I'd been doing.

For the physical I did some basic movements like walk up three steps and back down and I turned my head and coughed. Then the doctor hooked me up to run the EKG and the machine spit out the results.

He came back to me with a concerned look on his face. "We found some irregularities on your EKG. We're going to need to run some more tests."

I couldn't believe it. I'd finally warmed up to the idea of being a cop, and now even being able to enter the academy was already a struggle.

My mom took me back to the same office where the doctor told me nothing was wrong. This time we saw the older doctor and he did another EKG and ran more tests.

Now, we sat in a sterile room with one of those skinny doctor beds with paper on it and pictures of the beach and ocean on the wall. The doctor came in with the younger female doctor in tow. "I want you to see what you missed," he said to her.

I instantly realized that this was a bad sign and something was wrong with me. I listened as the doctor went into an explanation that consisted of words like electrodes and supraventricular tachycardia and atrioventricular node. My head was swimming and I tried hard to understand what was wrong.

My mom asked questions, and the answers led to more questions. I finally learned that It looked like I'd had two mild heart attacks and my heart rate had gotten as high as 350 beats per minute! I had something called Wolff-Parkinson White syndrome where extra electrodes create more pathways between the atria and the ventricles. These extra pathways made my heart contract way too fast.

Luckily, there was a fairly new procedure called Radiofrequency Catheter Ablation that would most likely fix it. The doctor suggested that we wait to do the surgery until after the New Year. It's funny now, but this was 1999, and back then Y2K was the big worry. People were storing food and water in shelters and preparing for the end. We really didn't know what would happen with our new computerized world when the clock struck midnight and we began a new century.

"Why don't we go ahead and do the surgery a little earlier so we know that we actually have electricity to do it," my mom had said.

The doctor couldn't argue with that, so much sooner than I expected I found myself heading to the hospital with a stomach full of nerves.

The doctor had gone over the procedure with me and I'd tried to be cool about it, but they were going to stick wires into my neck at my Carotid artery that would snake down to my heart and then burn the extra electrodes. The thought of that was bad enough, but then I was told I'd have to be awake during it.

I didn't know if I should be cussing at John or thanking him for talking me into the police academy.

Maybe it saved my life, but as I walked through the hospital doors I sure the hell didn't want to be there.

Chapter 23

The nurse jabbed the IV into my arm and I tried to remain relaxed while lying on the hospital bed in a special room called an EP lab. I'd worked hard to mentally prepare myself for this, but the idea of having my heart basically burned was just a little bit troubling.

I was given some medication through the IV that would help me relax. My neck and chest were shaved and I was cleansed with an antiseptic. Then I was given a shot where they would insert the wire into my neck. It burned at first, but I took the pain and acted as if it was nothing.

A sterile sheet was draped over me and the doctor reiterated that I had to remain completely still during the surgery and I should never lift my head up to see what is happening.

"If you feel too much pain, let me know," the nurse said.

"Okay," I replied.

"Ready?" the doctor asked.

I didn't know if I was ready or not, but I didn't exactly have a choice. "I'm good," I said.

The doctor made an incision in my neck and slid the wire inside. The incision area was numb, but I could feel the wire moving. The doctor checked the monitors that I was hooked up to as he made adjustments.

"Doing okay?" the nurse asked.

"Yes."

"Okay, we're in place," the doctor said. "You may feel your heart beating stronger or faster than usual and you might feel some burning."

The doctor went to work and I felt all of the above. He asked me questions about what I felt and I told him. It hurt a little bit, and then it hurt more, and then I got a strong burning smell in my nostrils. I started to say something to the nurse about it when I noticed little tendrils of smoke rising from my face. I realized it was actually coming from my nostrils and for a moment I thought I'd freak out.

Instead, I tried to remain relaxed and told myself that I'd be alright. Eventually, the surgery ended and the wires were removed. It felt like worms were being sucked from my body as the wires were pulled from my neck.

I was on bed rest for the afternoon and hooked up to special monitors that tracked my heartbeat. I had to lay still and wait to find out the actual results of the surgery. Of course we hoped it would be a one hundred percent success, but there was a chance I'd be stuck taking medication for the rest of my life or I could even have to wear a pacemaker.

When I saw my mom she gave me a worried look. "How was it?" she asked.

"It hurt," I said in a much more timid voice than I wanted.

"I'm sorry," she replied. "It's going to be okay though."

She was right. We got back the results and the surgery worked perfectly. I was healed and I would not need medication or a pacemaker.

John had gotten into the police academy and he continued to tell me how it was. Now that I had gone through hell to get in I was even more focused, but I had to wait until the next class.

Finally, the time came and I entered the police academy. If somebody told me two years earlier when I was dealing drugs that I'd be taking this step I would have laughed at them and then sold them a dime bag.

Chapter 24

Despite my desire to become a policeman, I was still young at just 18 years old. I didn't take the academic side of the academy seriously, probably a holdover from my days in high school and continuation school. I treated the physical part like a game. I just wanted to be the best at everything, the best at athletics, the best shooter, the best driver, and didn't care why or how. Sometimes I pissed off my instructors and they told me I was just playing cop instead of trying to learn.

Looking back on it, I know it was stupid. I should have been more focused on actually learning. After six months I still graduated, but academically I was like 44th out of a class of 52.

It was now the middle of 2000 and I was almost 19 years old. I had my POST (Police Officer Standards and Training) certificate and I was ready to get out there and be a bad ass cop.

I sent off my application to a couple of departments and then waited and waited. It was a ridiculously slow process, and in the mean time I continued to do jiu jitsu and then even got into mixed martial arts training. I did it to stay in shape because when the first couple of departments interviewed me they asked what I'd been doing for fitness.

The training at the academy was really rigorous, but afterward a lot of cops got lazy. It was so bad that they were actually giving out bonuses for staying within the specified weight.

I wasn't going to let myself get fat and lazy, so I started training while waiting to get hired on as a cop. Unfortunately, the first two police departments told me that I was just too young. I should come back in a couple years when I turn 21.

I applied with another department and then another and 2000 turned into 2001. I kept getting the same response. "You're too young."

I became more and more disgruntled with the process. Why was I able to join the academy at 18 if I wouldn't be able to get a job until I was 21? And my POST was only good for three years. Why didn't the academy tell me when I applied? I got the feeling that they didn't care and just wanted my money. I got a sour taste in my mouth that became bitterer with each rejection.

The gym where I'd been training, Pacific Martial Arts, was owned by my friend Matt Smith. I'd trained with him off and on since way back during my karate days. He knew how frustrated I was getting with the job search and one day after a hard session of kickboxing he said, "Hey, why don't you think of actually fighting?"

"Yeah, I'll think about it," I said in a non-committal tone.

"It will be a way to make some money and you have the talent for it."

"I don't know, maybe," I replied with a shrug.

Even though I was so pissed about the hiring process, I continued to apply and I didn't think I really wanted to get in a cage and fight somebody.

Besides, I'd just turned 20 and I was getting closer to being old enough to become a cop.

Then just a week and a half after my 20th birthday, 9/11 happened and our country was in shock. At that point I thought fuck being a cop. I'm joining the military. I'd come from a military family and I was ready to serve my country.

I signed up for the Army and I was hungry to join, but I got rejected. My Wolff-Parkinson syndrome that led to the heart surgery two years earlier kept me out. I was crushed, and my mom called our congressman and he tried to help me out. Unfortunately, not even he could get an exception. I was so tired of rejection and I was ready to say screw it all and get back into dealing drugs to start making big money like I'd done before.

Then a decision was made for me that would change my life.

Chapter 25

Pacific Martial Arts is your typical gym, an open space with blue mats, a bunch of hanging heavy bags, grappling dummies stacked along another wall, and a big metal fan that helps circulate the sweat-soaked air.

It was a pretty simple gym with a constant smell of sweat and a sense of commitment. Mats and bags and willing training partners were all we needed.

I was in my blue BJJ Gi with a shirt with the word TapouT stretched across the front of it underneath. I'd recently met Mask, one of the owners of Tapout, and he along with his buddies Punkass and Skyscrape had started their t-shirt company out of the trunk of their car in the mid-90s. They were helping fighters all through California by giving us gear and clothing.

I was adjusting the fan when I saw a guy in a gray suit walk through the door. I headed over to him thinking he was a customer. "Hey, what can I do for you? How can I help you?" I asked.

"I came to drop off these flyers," he held up a stack of flyers in his hand. Then, to my surprise he said, "Is Cole here?"

"Yeah...I'm Cole," I replied.

"Oh, okay, cool. I was just making sure that you were training and ready for your fight next weekend."

"I uh, I think you must be mistaken. I'm not fighting next weekend."

"You're Cole Escovedo right?"

"Uh huh, but I don't know about any fight."

"Yeah, Matt Smith signed you up for a fight next weekend."

I kind of shook my head back and forth trying to wrap my brain around what this guy was telling me. He continued. "We needed a replacement because a guy was in a car wreck and his head went through a windshield. Matt said you were our man."

"Oh well, awesome, news to me..."

A worried look crossed his face.

"I mean, I'll do it," I said. "It's just that I'm kind of surprised."

"Great, we're looking forward to having you fight for us. I'm Reed Harris, by the way." He smiled and stuck out his hand. "We have a new promotion called World Extreme Cagefighting. This is our second show. It's in Lemoore at The Palace."

We talked a little more and he gave me more specifics. I'd be fighting a guy named Terry Dull. Then he gave me the flyers and told me he'd see me in a few days.

As I sat the flyers down on the front counter in the reception area I felt a little shell-shocked. I glanced down at them again. They were advertising WEC 2 featuring "The Giant" Gan McGee. I'd remembered watching him fight in the UFC just a few months earlier.

A little later, Matt arrived at the gym. "When were you going to tell me?" I asked.

He got a shit-eating grin on his face. "How'd you find out?"

"Reed Harris came by to drop off some flyers and asked me if I was ready to fight."

"So you'll do it?"

"I told him I would."

"I think it will be good for you, Cole."

Matt was the type of guy to do something like that. He always wanted to push us outside of our comfort zone. He had a degree in psychology and he was always into those mind games to challenge others.

He definitely challenged me. I'd been in a little bit of a funk because of the police deal and then being unable to join the Army after 9/11. I'd stayed away from getting back into dealing, but other than that I was stuck. Now, I had a whole new thing to think about. In less than a week's time I would be getting in a cage and fighting somebody I didn't even know.

Chapter 26

My hands had just been wrapped by somebody I didn't know. I sat in a chair across from my mom and extended and flexed my fingers. I was in our designated area outside at The Palace waiting for Dave Camarillo. He was coming to corner me, but he hadn't made it yet. It was just my mom and me.

Across the room there was a guy that had about six inches and twenty or thirty pounds on me. He wore shorts and a t-shirt and he pounded away on some Thai pads. The pop of his foot against the pads sounded like gunshots. I'd just learned that he was Terry Dull, the guy I'd be fighting. He looked lightning fast as he kicked the shit out of the pads.

I glanced at my mom. "Wow, I think this might have been a mistake," I said.

"We can leave whenever you want," she replied.

She obviously didn't want me to fight, but as always she supported me because she knew it was something I wanted to do. "You know, you don't HAVE to do this. We can get up and leave right now. Nobody is going to stop us from leaving. We can go."

"No, I'm here. I said I'd do it and I'll go through with it. I don't care."

It was kind of like I was talking myself into it. It really was something I needed to prove to myself. All through elementary school and high school I was the one who was getting beaten up. I had to do this to see what I was really made of, to see if I could take a punch and give a punch. As I glanced up at Terry Dull I knew that I was going to find out really fast.

Dave still wasn't there and it was almost time for me to fight. I later learned he was stuck in a traffic jam. "Mom, you're going to have to corner me," I said as I threw punches and kicks at the air.

"What's a corner?"

I stopped and gave her a quick explanation.

"Okay, I'll corner you," she said.

A moment later, a guy stuck his head through an opening in the tent and told us it was time to fight. I walked toward the cage with my mom by my side. We were the first fight and The Palace was maybe half full. I think half of the attendees were probably already a little tipsy. There was sporadic clapping and I noticed some giant trophies next to the cage. They stood at least five feet tall and I liked the idea of winning one, but my repaired heart was beating at about 9,000 beats per minute and my arms and legs felt heavy. I thought there was a chance I might blow chunks before getting to the cage because my stomach was twisting in knots.

An official checked me over and made sure I had a mouthpiece and cup, and then I stood in the cage across from a man that had at least ten years on me and stood almost a head taller.

My name was announced and I raised my hand. More sporadic clapping. I glanced down at my mom. She looked a little worried, but determined as well. She always was a fighter.

Terry Dull was announced. He raised his hand and looked through the cage toward the front row. I followed his line of sight. He was looking at his wife and kid.

My racing heart and twisting stomach built to a fever pitch until the referee told us to fight. As soon as I walked forward toward this kickboxer who wanted to beat the shit out of me, the nerves vanished.

I was ready for this. I needed to prove to myself that I had it in me. Then he punched me in the jaw and kicked me in my ribs. I brought my hands up and tried to fire back, but I was hit again and again. I backed up. I circled. He pressed forward. Everything was happening at a crazy pace.

Finally, I remembered what I was good at. I ducked under a punch and locked him up. I dragged him to the ground and he ended up in my guard. This didn't stop him from trying to punch my nose into my brain. He swung wildly.

I thought I heard my mom screaming, "What the hell! Get the hell off of him!"

She'd been in bar fights, but didn't know what to expect with this whole cage fighting thing.

Terry Dull swung at me again. I threw my legs up and popped my hips. In an instant I had him locked in a triangle. The punching stopped as he struggled to escape.

I squeezed tighter and he was forced to tap. In just under two minutes it was over. I'd won my first fight.

Dull kind of rolled to the side as I released the triangle. His arms and legs seemed locked up in a weird bent position, like a turtle on its back. The doctor and referee were over him and I bent down to tell him good fight and thank him.

"I can't move. " I heard him say in a panicked voice.

As I stood in the cage with a tornado of contrasting emotions he was taken away on a stretcher. I was sure I had paralyzed him for life in front of his wife and kid. It was the total worst case scenario.

Even after receiving my trophy and then an unexpected five hundred dollars, I wasn't sure if this sport was for me. I couldn't stomach the idea that I had possibly ruined a man's life.

My mom, who had given Dull's wife her business card so she could let her know how he was doing, looked at me. "You've got your damn trophy. That's it. You just paralyzed a man. You can't do this!"

I fully agreed with her.

A day after the fight I learned that I had dislocated Dull's neck. He had a pre-existing back injury and the triangle hit him just right. He would spend a long time in a hospital, but he'd recover.

The adrenaline heading into the fight and the brief moment of elation after winning felt absolutely awesome. After seeing Dull laying there on the canvas and the looks on his wife's and kid's faces, I was still unsure if I wanted to fight again.

"I just don't want to do this. It's not for me. I don't want to be responsible for crippling some guy in front of his family," I told Matt when I saw him in the gym later that day.

"No, no," he said. "It's not like that. He's not paralyzed. Don't worry. That was just a fluke."

Looking back now and considering the safety record of MMA, I know that it really was a fluke.

We talked a lot more about it and Matt asked me how I felt before, during, and after the fight. I had to admit that it was a complete thrill and I was proud of myself for doing it.

Despite my concern for Dull and his family, I finally decided that I would give it another try. My mom wasn't so happy about that decision.

Chapter 27

Mike Popp is a former police officer who had gotten into jiu jitsu after retiring. I'd met him at Pacific Martial Arts and gravitated toward him because of my interest about becoming a cop. We'd become good friends and he'd been working with me more and more. I felt like we really clicked and after my first fight he became really focused on helping me.

Mike told me that his buddy at Ultimate Athlete, a nationwide magazine, had taken photos. "You should go by their office and get some shots. It'd be cool to have them," Mike had said.

I entered their offices and told them why I was there. The guy I needed to talk to was on the phone. He came out a minute later. "Cool, I've got some photos for you, Cole." He started to turn, but then paused as if an idea had just popped into his head. "Hey, you want to go fight in Indiana next month?"

"I'm just here to pick up some photos," I replied.

"I know, but we're putting on our first show out in Indiana. We've had a couple guys drop out."

I shrugged my shoulders. "I guess I could."

"Awesome!"

"Will I get paid for it?"

"Definitely, we'll pay for your flight and hotel room and we'll give you a thousand dollars."

I was all for that. It was a big raise from my last fight and I was young and ready for the adventure. I'd planned on just picking up some photos and I'd ended up with my second fight.

I headed back to the gym and told Mike and Matt the news. They were both happy about it and Mike wanted to be my trainer for the fight. It made sense to me, and he got focused on preparing me for my second MMA venture.

The disappointments of not being able to become a cop or enlist in the Army were now in my rear view mirror. The thoughts of getting back into dealing drugs were right there with them. I was now totally focused on being a fighter except for the one distraction of a girl who I'd been off and on with for a long time.

Every now and then she'd pop back in my life, and as I prepared for my fight with a guy named Bart Palaszewski, she showed up. She wasn't around for long, and I didn't let her derail my training.

On January 27, 2002, I found myself in Hammond, Indiana at the Hammond Civic Center. The arena had a basketball gymnasium feel to it with a wall surrounding the main floor and a second floor on top of the wall.

I stood in the cage as maybe a thousand people looked on. Bart Palaszewski stood across from me. He was a member of Jeff Curran's team locally, and I was definitely an outsider. As I stared across the cage I thought he seemed young and nervous as well.

The ring girl stood by me and she reeked of Jack Daniels. I asked Matt to get rid of her.

The referee finally told us to start and we hooked it up. I jumped on Bart and landed a bunch of good shots. In just over two minutes the fight was over and my hand was raised. I'd won my second fight and a real feeling of accomplishment washed over me. I was 2-0 and it felt damn good.

Chapter 28

Over the next six months or so I focused solely on fighting. Mike and Brad Alcorn trained me and I ripped through my next two opponents, Jay Valencia and Paul Morris, both in under a minute. The submission win over Valencia wasn't really noteworthy, but what happened afterward is.

As mentioned, my mom and dad had run with a motorcycle club for years when they were younger. Some of my other family members were high ranking members of the Mongols MC. I was the first fight of the night, and just before it started about 75 members of the Mongols showed up. Some of them were passing around just outside of the metal detector.

My mom told Steve that she wasn't okay with it. He agreed, and had a tec-9 in the trunk of his car, but it was half an acre away in the parking lot.

I was hitting pads with my cornerman, Brad Alcorn. He was a homicide detective and trained at the gym. My mom showed up with a worried look on her face. She told us about the Mongols. "Listen Cole, you know you have some high-ranking relatives with the Mongols. If anybody recognizes your name and wants to talk to you, don't do it."

I shrugged. "No problem, Mom. I won't talk to them."

She then turned to Brad. "They've been at war with the Hells Angels so who knows what could go down."

Brad opened up his bag and pulled out his 45. "Everything will be okay," he grinned.

"Good," my mom said. "I think Steve and I are leaving after your fight. Are you okay with that?"

"Yeah, that's okay. I'll stay out of trouble." I assured her.

During my fight the Mongols sat behind my mom and Steve with colors on and chanting their club song, but there wasn't any trouble.

After my win, I changed and hung out in the crowd watching the fights. Everything was good until the main event when Rick Slaton fought Leo Pavlushkin. Slaton was a Mongol and the reason his biker gang buddies were there.

The bikers were going crazy, and then Slaton threw a knee that apparently caught Pavlushkin in the nuts. He doubled over and struggled to recover. The Mongols got pissed at having to wait. They started throwing beer cups towards the cage. I was sitting just one section over, and I saw a guy get hit with a cup of beer. He was pissed, and picked it up and fired it back at the gang.

This of course was a really bad idea.

The Mongols stormed up to him and his friends and they exchanged words. Then bam, one of the gang members busted him in the head and the fight was on. This led to other fights breaking out, and it became a free-for-all with fists and chairs flying across the room. People got beat to hell and three people got stabbed.

The police showed up in full force and I got out of there.

The FBI got involved and I was even asked to make a declaration about what I saw. I never heard from them afterward though. Years later it came out that an ATF agent named William Queen was undercover after infiltrating the Mongols. He was at the fights, and eventually wrote a book about his time under cover. The Ultimate Athlete riot was actually in it.

Crazy shit, but I got a win and got out without getting stabbed.

I was 4-0 and fully into being a professional fighter.

My life had taken a crazy turn over the previous six months, and it was about to take another one. The girl I mentioned before turned up once again, and she was pregnant. I thought back to that one damn night when she'd returned.

She argued with me. "You won't have anything to do with the baby. It's not even yours," she told me in front of my house one day.

I'd lost my dad to prison, and even though I didn't like the idea of having a kid while I was so young, I wasn't going to lose my child.

"Take a paternity test," I told her.

"No, I'm not doing that," she replied.

This went on for a few days until my mom had finally had enough. "We'll get a court order for the test," she said.

About the time we were filing the papers, I got on a plane for Denver, Colorado. Ultimate Athlete was holding its third event in the Mile High

City. I'd fought on their first two cards and they really wanted me back. Now I was becoming something of a draw and had gained a little bit of a following with my fast 4-0 start.

I met up with Christian Allen. He was a huge home town favorite. I'd dominated my first four fights, but I was unable to put Allen away early. For the first time ever I had to go to the second round. My lungs were on fire and my arms and legs felt like tree trunks as I struggled to suck in the thin Denver air. I was totally gassed and thought I might have to tap, but I managed to reach deep and catch him with a good shot and then stop him with punches.

I was 5-0 and feeling great despite the struggles with my old girlfriend and the fact that I might be a dad soon.

About a month after returning from Denver the court agreed that she had to take the test. Just days after the court's decision, I got a call from Reed Harris. The WEC wanted me to fight for its first ever featherweight title. "Who will I be fighting?" I asked.

"Philip Perez," Reed replied.

Oh shit. This is going to be crazy, I thought. Philip Perez was from our rival gym where there were gang ties.

"Are you in?" Reed asked.

"Hell yeah, let's do it," I said.

Chapter 29

Once word of the fight got out the Fresno fight community went insane. It was seen as the measuring stick between the two gyms. When Philip Perez and I met at WEC 5 for the inaugural featherweight belt it would tell us which gym was the best.

Our gym, Pacific Martial Arts, had a bunch of cops training at it. I knew most of them from the academy or through Mike Popp. We had a close group of guys who trained hard and looked out for each other.

Philip Perez's gym was across town and it was the first true fight gym in the area. That was all they did, fight. There was no specific martial art training. And some of the guys who trained there were gang members.

It was the perfect grudge match. On the one hand you had the more traditional gym where many of Fresno's finest trained, and on the other you had a bunch of fighting gangsters. Each gym was sending their guy to settle it in the cage.

It had been three days since news of the fight got out. Mike and I had just finished a hard training session that focused on takedowns from the clinch. My rash guard was soaked with sweat and I grabbed a towel to wipe my face down as two plainclothes cops who trained from time to time entered the gym.

They made their way over to where Mike and I were standing. "What's up Jackson, Mendez," Mike said.

"We heard about the fight with Perez," Jackson said.

"Yeah, it's going to be a good one," Mike replied.

"Listen, this guy is no joke. He's reportedly a member of the Bulldogs."

"I know," I said. "I'll be ready."

"Keep your eyes open. He isn't some average Joe and there are active gang members at their gym."

"I understand. Thanks for the heads up."

We talked a little longer and then I went to grab a shower. I'd started bouncing at a local sports bar and had to get over there for my shift. I'd been working there since right before my first fight. I figured, screw it, if I was going to be a fighter I might as well get paid to bounce too.

On the way to the bar I briefly thought about the warning. I knew that this Perez guy was a gang member and there were a lot of rough fuckers running around Fresno, but I didn't think too much about it. A fight was a fight and we'd get in the cage and do our thing. No matter what the outcome was I didn't think I'd get shit from his gang.

The shift started pretty slow and I helped check ID's at the door. At around ten at night, two straight up thugs walked up. They wore white shirts and baggy, dark blue jeans with bandanas sticking out of the pockets. One of them had a tattoo on his neck, I think it was a dagger, and the other had a prison tat on his face.

Again, I thought about the warning from earlier in the day, but I couldn't let that bother me. "ID's gentlemen," I said.

They pulled out their ID's and I gave a quick look before handing them back.

"You Cole Escovedo, right?" one of them said.

It wasn't a good thing for guys like them to know who you were. "Yeah, I'm Cole," I replied in a neutral tone.

"Oh shit, Philip is gonna fuck you up good. You know that right?"

I shrugged. "Guess we'll see on the 18th."

"Fuck yeah we'll see, Pendejo. We'll see you knocked the fuck out."

"You going to come in and drink or keep running your mouth?" I asked.

Now the other one spoke up. "You going to get shot. If somehow you win we going to shoot your punk ass and we going to shoot up your gym too."

By now, another bouncer had showed up. "Sorry guys, we're full. You've got to go."

"We don't want to drink in this bitch place no how."

Then he called me a bunch of names like bitch and pussy and stuck his finger toward my face.

I let him run his mouth for a moment before simply saying, "Alright, goodnight then."

They left, and then circled around the parking lot real slow. I thought they might pull out a gun and try to shoot me right there, but instead they drove away. Maybe they really thought that Philip was going to beat my ass, but I definitely had other plans.

It was the worst case scenario and I realized I had gotten myself into some deep shit, but there was no way in hell I was going to puss out. Despite the consistent threats and continually looking over my shoulder, I trained my ass off so I could beat up Philip Perez, gangster or not, at WEC 5 on October 18, 2002.

Chapter 30

There was a pretty heavy police presence at the weigh-in, and other than some shit-talking nothing went down. Now, I stood in a makeshift room and focused on my game plan for fighting Philip Perez. Jeff Bedard and Antonio Banuelos were about to fight, and then it would be my turn.

At the time The Palace held its events in a big tent out back. The place was swarming with police officers because they were sure that one way or another there would be trouble. They even had metal detectors to check people at the door.

Bedard scored a quick submission via a Guillotine and I could almost feel the crowd's anticipation for my fight.

I followed the three bikini-clad girls as they led me toward the cage through the smoke and a screaming audience. I couldn't believe the intensity in the room. There were the guys from Perez's gym booing me and calling me names, and then the guys from my gym cheering for me.

Philip Perez was already there, waiting for me. His left arm was full of tattoos and *Team Fresno* was scrawled across his chest. His manager was Terry Dull, the first guy I fought, and he carried Perez's IFC belt around the cage. This one was for the IFC belt and the inaugural WEC belt.

Paul Smith, who ran the IFC, and I had a little argument months earlier. It wasn't a big deal, but I made a point to approach him and apologize. He appreciated the effort and decided he would use our bout to unify the two belts.

Perez glared at me like he wanted to push my nose into my brain as the announcer Jeff Weller, whose face was painted in KISS makeup complete with blood coming from his lips for the Halloween-themed event, announced my name.

I pulled off my Karate Gi and undershirt while Weller introduced me. I looked across the cage at Perez. It was like a volcano was seconds away from erupting. So much trash talk had flown back and forth leading to the fight, and as I stood in the cage amidst the screaming crowd I was ready to let loose.

Dave Camarillo and Brad Alcorn, who besides being a detective was also married to boxer Jennifer Alcorn, were in my corner. I glanced at them and Brad offered me some water. I didn't need it.

The referee held his arms out toward each of us and I bowed toward Perez and then toward the referee. He returned an odd half bow and Perez and I took that as permission to fight. We both quickly headed toward each other like two dogs being let off a short leash. The referee stopped us and pushed us back. He wasn't quite ready.

The crowd grew louder and seconds later the referee gave us the go ahead. We met in the middle of the cage and I immediately fired off a jab that dropped Perez to his knees. It was just a flash knockdown and he shot for the takedown. He was in my guard and I was fine with that.

He tried to stay busy and worked us toward the fence. I worked to tie up his left arm and immediately started looking for subs. I went for a triangle but didn't have it. Perez lifted me up and dropped me next to the fence.

I tied up his arms as he tried to land shots from the top. Then I saw an opening for an armbar. Again, Perez lifted me up and I was unable to lock it in. He continued to try to work from the top and landed a couple shots, but nothing that hurt. We scrambled, and I reversed him and spun to side control.

He tried for an armbar and I pulled out of it. Back on our feet, we exchanged a couple times and he connected with a left. I motioned for him to bring it on, and pushed forward. He backed up and I threw a head kick that found its mark. Perez fell into the fence, dazed. I rushed forward, but he bounced off the fence and shot for a double leg.

He was in my guard and I could tell he was using the time to recover. I remained calm and kept searching for an opening. I finally got it and slid my legs up to Perez's neck. I locked up the triangle and knew that I had it. He was crouched to my left and I reached for his head and shifted my legs to drop him to his knees.

He tapped and fell onto his back. I jumped up. The referee thought I was still going after Perez. I shrugged him off and helped Perez to his feet. We hugged, and then I ran across the cage and climbed the fence in celebration.

It was only a little over a year earlier when I had my first fight. Now I was the champ.

Jeff Weller announced me as the winner. My hand was raised and Reed Harris put the belt around my waist.

Ryan Bennett interviewed me and asked me how I felt. "I'm feeling great. I'm feeling all that hard work paid off. I'm proof tonight, all you who doubt yourself...train hard, believe in yourself, and you will win! It's as simple as that."

Ryan asked about the bad blood and wanted to know how I felt about it now. "All I want to say is Team Fresno, Philip Perez, I respect you brother. I respect you more than I ever thought I would."

When asked what was next, I said that I was ready to really make a career out of it. And then I posed for a photo with Scott Adams and Reed Harris, and Paul Smith from the IFC congratulated me.

I left the cage and felt as if I was walking on air. I'd done it. I'd become the champ. I didn't think anything could stop this feeling, but then the next morning the paternity test came in the mail. My brother came over to me and said, "Bummer, Bro, the party's over."

Chapter 31

How in the hell was I going to be a dad? That's the question that kept rolling through my mind leading to Gabby's birth. I was pissed at myself and at my ex-girlfriend. I was only 21 years old and my future was unfolding in a cage. Now I had a baby to be responsible for.

Gabby was a beautiful baby girl, and despite my worries about being a dad, I wanted to be in her life. My ex-girlfriend didn't want me to be involved though and we went back and forth with each other.

As I trained for my next fight, my mom and I fought for my rights to spend time with my daughter. In February of 2003, I met Noah Shinable at Gladiator Challenge 14 and finished him in less than two minutes with the move I was now known for, the Triangle.

I was now 7-0 and held two belts. I felt as if I was nearly unbeatable. I was on top of the world. The struggle for partial custody of Gabby seemed to be going in our favor as well.

Nothing could derail me, so that's why just six weeks after beating Shinable I was back in the cage. This time I fought Bao Quach. He had a wrestling background and I think we both expected the fight to be on the ground. We ended up going to town on our feet and blasting away at each other. I had the reach, but Bao was tough as hell.

Early on in round one he landed a good shot to my eye. I felt something give. I tried to shake it off, but I had double vision. I continued to fight and we had many big exchanges. I was unsure if I won or lost the first round.

Round two was much of the same. Early on I landed a big shot and my hand started throbbing. I guessed that I had broken it, but I kept throwing it. After round two, I was again unsure if I had won it or not.

This had turned into my toughest fight yet, and I knew that I had to go all out and look for a finish in the third. As I walked back to my corner people started piling into the cage. "What's going on?" I asked the referee.

"Fight's over," he replied.

"Why," I said. "I'm fine."

"It was a two-rounder."

What in the hell! We were the main event of a mega-fight card. Why would it just be two rounds? A moment later, I stood in the center of the cage and waited for the decision to be read.

I'd finished my first seven fights, and standing there waiting for a decision was like waiting at a doctor's office without anything to do. It seemed to take forever, and then finally the decision was announced. "Bao Quach!" the announcer yelled.

I congratulated him and felt numb inside. I'd been beaten. I was the champ. I was undefeated. I'd destroyed almost every one of my previous opponents, and now I had lost.

I made my way through the crowd back to my locker room. With each step, fury built inside of me. If only I would have known it was a two-round fight, I thought. Why the hell did I not know that?

My vision was still jacked up and my hand pulsed with pain. I pushed through the door into the locker room and lost it. I tipped over a table and picked up a chair and flung it across the room. I punched the wall and I let out a growling yell. My corner, the guys I trained with on a daily basis, tried to console me. It didn't work.

I paced the room and blasted anything in my way. How the fuck could I have lost? My mom arrived. She tried to calm me down as well. Finally, the anger started to subside. I picked up a chair and plopped down into it.

Bao Quach came into the room. I looked up at him and saw his face was swollen and bruised. "Cole, I just wanted to check on you to see how you're doing."

I stood. "I'm alright. Great fight," I said.

"You too."

"We're about to go to the hospital," my mom said. "I think you need to get checked up too."

Bao smiled through swollen lips. "I will."

Despite my frustration and anger, this moment illustrated what the California fight scene was all about back then. Even though we tried our best to beat the crap out of each other, we still recognized that we were part of a small group. In some ways other fighters, even the ones we fought against, were something like an extended family.

At the hospital over the next few hours I learned that I had a Boxer's fracture in my hand and a broken orbital bone. It was a long night and I ended up needing a metal plate in my hand and reconstructive surgery on my orbital.

I'd tasted defeat for the first time and it was bitter and painful. I was sidelined for a while and I had a lot of time to think. I wondered if I really should keep fighting. After all, I was now a dad and I was young. But then I got a call from the WEC. They wanted me to defend my belt. Despite the doctor telling me it would be better if I waited, I accepted the fight. I'd realized that I had to do it. Fighting was in my blood.

Chapter 32

It was almost exactly a year after I won my WEC belt before I had the chance to defend it. My fights with Noah Shinable and Bao Quach had been in Gladiator Challenge. At WEC 8 I met up with Anthony Hamlett.

It was just six months after my fight with Quach and the doctors advised me to wait a little longer. I couldn't do it though. I had to get back in the cage to wash away the sting of the decision loss. For my first fight against Terry Dull I felt like I had to get in there to prove something to myself. Now it felt like I had to prove something to myself all over again.

Hamlett would be tough, and I trained hard to fight him. But it was odd because my opponent was almost an afterthought. It didn't matter who was on the other side of the cage. I had to get it in there and fight for myself.

Jeff Weller was decked out in costume once again, and the crowd was rowdy. Not as much so as my fight with Philip Perez, but still rowdy. And speaking of Perez, after I beat him things went bad for Fresno Fight Team. Literally like a month after our fight their gym closed down. Many of their members came to our gym, and one of them was Perez.

He came to Pacific Martial Arts and asked if it was cool for him to train with us.

"Sure," I replied. "If you're coming in with the attitude of wanting to train and learn and fight for your team like it is your family, because we are like a family."

He assured our coaches and me that he was ready to do that.

"Then we're happy to have you," I said.

He did have that attitude and it was cool to see him in our gym training after all the shit that had gone down before we fought. He fought a couple times as a member of Pacific Martial Arts and I even cornered him in one of the fights.

He'd become part of our family.

At WEC 8, Anthony Hamlett was not part of our family. I badly wanted to finish him so I could gain a little of what I had lost after my fight with Quach. The first round was back and forth. It took me a little bit to settle in, but once I did I felt good.

Early in the second round I rocked him and landed a bunch of unanswered shots. The fight was stopped and I earned the TKO victory. I'd defended my featherweight title and shook off a little bit of the loss to Quach. I felt that I was back on track.

Only days after the Hamlett fight I found myself in a car on the bad side of town. My ex, Gabby's mom, was in between apartments and had temporarily moved to the bad side of Fresno. We're talking a part of town that isn't even safe for an adult, let alone a baby. She and I had talked and decided that it would be best if I took Gabby for a while.

The area was so bad that it was not a good idea to go there alone, so I asked my mom and Steve to come along just to be safe.

It made sense that Gabby come stay with me while my ex got everything sorted out, and I wanted to be in my girl's life.

We picked her up without being mugged and headed back home. I was excited and nervous because I understood that it was fully my job to care for her. It was time to be both a fighter and a dad.

Chapter 33

My ex came by a couple days after I'd gotten Gabby. She didn't have much to say. Instead, she just dropped off the rest of Gabby's things. They didn't amount to much, only a couple bags.

It seemed she had resigned herself to the fact that she was giving up her daughter for at least the time being. It was a hard thing to see. Even though I'd been pissed off at her for a long time I still wanted her to be there for Gabby.

I got back to training while building a relationship with my baby girl. She was so cute and sweet and I wanted her to be around me, but I also needed to spend a lot of time in the gym. I had two belts to defend.

Every now and then my mom would watch her, but she also bought a playpen for me to take to the gym. She reasoned that if I was going to be up there all the time Gabby needed to be up there as well.

The months rolled by since my title defense against Hamlett and I had two fights lined up that ended up falling through. Then I got a couple injuries that pushed me back a bit.

Gabby became the darling of the gym and she really took to Mike Popp and Doug Marshall. Doug is a muscled-up bald guy with tattoos all over his body. He'd fought on the WEC 8 card as well in his MMA debut. Then he blasted through his next few opponents in the upcoming months.

He was focused and hungry and he trained like a mad man. Gabby would watch Doug train as Mike yelled out instructions. Pretty soon, she started yelling instructions of her own. "Work harder Doug," she'd say, or, "More pushups Doug. You can do it."

It was hilarious, especially when Doug would do what she said and a smile would spread on her face.

Doug had been able to stay busy and fight a lot in 2004. It was a different story for me. Another fight fell through and I was completely frustrated. I even considered not fighting anymore, or at least taking an extended break, because of it. I'd established some positive routines with Gabby and we became closer and closer. I wondered if maybe I should forget about fighting and get a 'normal' job.

Then early in 2005, I got a fight in the IFC in Salt Lake City against Randy Spence. If this one fell through I decided I was done. A couple weeks before the fight, Gabby got sick. I took care of her while finishing up my camp, and then a week out I got sick too. I felt like complete hell, but there was no way I was backing out, so on March 5, 2005, I made the drive to Salt Lake City and climbed into the cage to take on Spence.

I went into the fight with a game plan of going for a knockout, but after being sick I decided that I needed to just focus on finding a way to finish as early as I could because I didn't know how much of a gas tank I'd have.

Spence had a lot of experience and had fought some tough guys, so as soon as the fight went to the ground I focused on searching for a submission and found my go-to sub, the triangle. I was really happy with the win, but I didn't have time to celebrate. I'd already signed the contract to fight Poppies Martinez in a little over two months, and it would be almost as crazy as the Philip Perez fight.

Chapter 34

I had just walked through the Tachi Palace where I took a little detour to see my slot machine. The Palace had done slot machines for its champions and mine was there. It was surreal and very cool. Now, I stood in the ring at a boxing event to promote next month's fight with Poppies Martinez.

You'd think a guy with a slot machine in the casino would have some fans, but not for this fight. Poppies was a member of the tribe. His nickname is actually "The Tachi Kid" and of course all the tribe members were pulling for him.

Over the last couple weeks we had exchanged harsh words. Poppies really didn't like me, and I wasn't sure why. Then I found out that he had tried to introduce himself to me and I didn't know who he was. This pissed him off. It was just an honest thing, I wasn't trying to be a dick, but he was still pissed.

The announcer asked us questions and we went back and forth a bit. He said something along the lines of how I couldn't fight and he was going to beat me. I got fired up and shot back with, "You're only saying this because you've been fed fights by the casino. You're their token guy. All you fight is garbage fighters."

Poppies didn't really appreciate this and he started to come after me. I was cool with that and met him halfway. His crew joined in and we scuffled a bit and it escalated quickly. Christian Printup, who worked as a promoter for the WEC, and Reed Harris struggled to break us apart. Finally, Reed pretty much wrapped his arms around me and threw me backward to get me out of it. To this day he jokes about how he threw me on my back and I did nothing about it.

After the scuffle, the animosity really heated up. I had been a great draw for Tachi Palace and they had treated me well, but now I was the villain. Poppies was their boy and everybody wanted him to win. It was so bad that Christian was even on the message boards talking bad about me. "How can you do that?" I asked him. "You're supposed to be promoting the fight, not bashing me."

Now I see that he felt he had to do it, and in a way he was promoting the fight. Leading up to WEC 15 if you weren't against me you were enemy number one.

Christian and I had been friends, but it got to the point where I didn't like him and I told him so. Later on, we made up and he is one of my good friends to this day, but before WEC 15 he and everybody else were against me.

This fueled my training and I was hungry to get in the cage and shut the crowd up. It would be my first fight at lightweight and I struggled to get up to the weight limit of 155 pounds. Poppies, on the other hand, was struggling to get down to 155. He even wanted to fight at 160. There was no way in hell I was doing that because he'd have a huge size advantage.

Finally, WEC 15 rolled around. It was May 19, 2005, and I stood in my trailer waiting to be given the signal to enter the arena.

Poppies had just been announced and the roar of the crowd was nearly deafening.

I got the word and my team and I headed for the cage. We had extra security encircling us because the pro-Poppies crowd was so hostile. Literally, almost everybody in the arena was against me except for a small group of my friends and family all sitting together in one section.

I was the champ and had been cheered many times in this very arena, now boos rained down on me as I entered the cage.

Poppies mean-mugged me from across the cage and I returned the stare. We were introduced and I was popping with energy. I'd had enough of the bullshit over the previous couple months. It had sat on my shoulders and I was ready to shrug it off by punching Poppies in the head repeatedly.

The referee told us to fight and we met in the center of the cage. I weighed around 150 pounds. I was sure Poppies was around 170. He'd finished most of his fights in a hurry, and I knew he'd look to do the same against me.

He came after me and we let our hands go in a flurry. He caught me with a couple good shots and I was surprised at how heavy his hands were. I've just got to weather the storm, I thought.

The pace was quick and we went back and forth. With each big flurry I could tell he was slowing down a bit. My plan was to wear him down, and despite being hit hard a few times, it was working. When we went to the ground I felt comfortable and didn't think he could submit me. I landed some solid shots from his guard.

Toward the end of the first round I could tell that he was starting to gas. I had trained hard and felt fine.

The second round started and I landed some good shots. He connected as well, but his punches didn't have as much sting.

I landed a leg kick and he stumbled. Before I even realized what was happening, the fight was over. Poppies couldn't continue because I'd blown out his knee. My emotions were like a wave crashing onto a jagged rock. I had a moment of complete anger and frustration and lost my composure for a split second. I'd won, but I wanted to finish decisively with a big KO or submission.

I regained myself and I was announced as the winner. The boos were thunderous and beer bottles and food were being thrown at us. The police escorted us back toward the trailer and the crowd was like an angry mob. They continued to throw shit at us and cussed us and spit at us, even the kids did all this! It was absolutely ridiculous.

It had been another tumultuous fight, but I'd come through it. Still, I was pissed at the way I was treated. I'm sure that the Palace wanted me to lose. That wasn't in my plans though, and now I had another title, the Native American Lightweight champ. Unfortunately, after beating Poppies I was never as well liked at The Palace as I had been before.

I was angry for having such a risk be forced on me, but it wouldn't be long before I'd be right back in the WEC cage.

Chapter 35

Now I was 10-1 and each fight carried more weight. More money was on the line and the fun was being drained. Fighting was now my job, and it was losing its appeal. I also had to think about Gabby and taking care of my family. I had to make money and I felt like I had to win. Again, I wondered how much longer I'd want to continue fighting. I mean there were parts of it that I absolutely loved, the challenge, the training, the friendships it created, but the business side of it weighed heavily on me.

It had been almost five months since I beat Poppies when I got a call from Reed Harris. We'd all kind of patched up the bad feelings and Reed needed a favor. "Can you step in to fight at lightweight against Joe Martin?"

I thought about it for a moment and decided that the right thing to do would be to accept. They needed me to help them out and this was a good way to show that I didn't hold any hard feelings, so at WEC 17 I was right back in the same arena where I had been cussed at and spit on just five months earlier.

My fight was buried in the middle of the card and the crowd wasn't anywhere near as hostile. Joe Martin, my opponent, wasn't their golden boy and I was still the WEC featherweight champ.

Almost immediately I landed a big head kick on Martin. He was rocked and I landed a few punches. We clinched, and I ended up really high on him. I jumped and locked up a flying triangle. He tried to fight it off, but I busted him with an elbow. This took the fight out of him and he tapped.

It was a crazy submission over a guy who had about twenty pounds on me because he couldn't even make 155. Some people were even saying it was sub of the year.

I felt good about this victory, but I didn't have long to savor it. A fight with Urijah Faber was in the works, but before that could happen some serious shit went down.

My previous fights and the recent high-profile submission had given me a certain level of fame in the Fresno area. It also made it where some guys thought they wanted to test their toughness out on me.

I was working at the bar not long after the fight with Martin when I was helping some drunken lunatic and he sucker punched me. I remained cool and tried to calm him after he hit me, but he threw another sloppy punch. I had to defend myself. I punched him in the face and that was the end of it.

Unfortunately, the punch basically caved his face in. He ended up having to get a metal plate inserted and then I started hearing from my police friends that there was a warrant for my arrest.

At the time, cage fighting still wasn't accepted as a sport by many people, and apparently the police chief and the Fresno politicians had decided to make an example out of me. They wanted to show that we were just a bunch of thugs who got in bar fights and that we weren't really athletes at all.

I got more calls from my police friends and they told me that this was serious because I was a fighter. They were treating me as a dangerous criminal who was to be approached with extreme caution.

My mom got an attorney and marched into the police chief's office demanding to know what was going on. He responded that he didn't know about any warrant, and this made things even stranger.

My mom thought that for some unknown reason they were looking for an opportunity to put a bullet in me. "Is there anything that could have happened that put you on the wrong side with somebody in the department?" my mom asked.

I thought about it and it just didn't make sense. I was friends with the cops. Then I thought that maybe the guy I busted up had some connections somewhere.

In any event, it was a stressful situation right before a huge fight.

I'd already talked with Josh Koscheck and he said I could train in his garage where it was safe. I did so, and tried to focus on training for Urijah, but the persistent worry made it hard.

Finally, my mom gave me five hundred dollars and I loaded up the car and headed to Nebraska to hopefully train in peace. I was temporarily leaving my life in Fresno behind. I didn't want to, but a guy with a broken face and a mysterious arrest warrant with some possibly trigger-happy police forced me to flee.

Chapter 36

After a couple weeks of being away I decided I had to get back to Fresno. My fight with Faber was right around the corner, and I wanted to see my daughter anyway. My cop friends had kept me up to date on the warrant, but really they didn't have much to report.

I had to get back and I had to get myself both physically and mentally prepared to fight, but I was a confused wreck. I didn't know if I'd walk toward the cage at The Palace and get hooked up by the cops.

I voiced my concerns of getting arrested to my mom. "Cole, they aren't going to hook you up there. The reservation is sovereign land. Besides, the WEC isn't going to let that happen. They want you to fight Urijah."

She was right, but the idea sat in the back of my head.

Despite my concern and uncertainty, I headed back home. Upon arrival, it seemed everything had worked itself out. The warrant was eventually dropped, and then I got a very interesting call from the International Fight League. They wanted me to fight former UFC champ Jens Pulver in Atlantic City.

This was a huge opportunity. The IFL was brand new and it had money and a lot of buzz behind it. I was getting a chance at a big fight on the

IFL's inaugural event. Even though my fight with Faber was just a week or so away I accepted the fight against Jens.

My plan was to beat Faber to retain my featherweight belt and then move to the big time against Pulver, so on March 17th of 2006 I headed to The Palace to take on Faber.

I stood across from him and the referee, Josh Rosenthal, pointed toward each of us and then said, "Fight!"

We met each other in the center of the cage and tapped gloves. There was a moment of calm, and then Faber drilled me with an overhand right and knocked me out for a moment. I was on my back and struggling to regain my senses. I looked up and saw Josh standing over me. Why the hell is Josh punching me, I thought? Then I realized it was Faber with his blond mop of hair that was all over me throwing punches and elbows.

He dragged me to the fence and I worked hard to keep him from landing any more blows. We stayed this way for a while until he dropped down for a heel hook. This gave me a chance to scramble on top and land some punches. I worked from there and popped Urijah with some solid punches and elbows. Then Faber shifted and we scrambled again. He ended up in my guard and went back to landing his own punches and elbows while I fought to defend myself and searched for a submission.

My forehead was swollen and my face was bruised, but Urijah had a nice knot under his right eye as well. Toward the end of the round I tried to lock in an armbar and then a triangle, but it wasn't happening.

Another elbow by Faber, and now the blood was flowing. I didn't know how badly I was cut, but the blood dumped into my eyes and I struggled to see.

More punches and elbows and I struggled to defend myself while staying busy from the bottom.

The round came to an end and I headed to my corner. The bleeding was stopped for the time being and I struggled to regain my faculties. I felt like I was still in the fight, but I also felt like I was getting the hell beat out of me. I couldn't believe this was happening. I knew he'd be tough, but not this tough. After accepting the Pulver fight I had already started filing this one away. Now I was in desperate need of something big to happen.

Round two started and I landed a hard leg kick. Just as I started to think that I could settle in and work on my feet for a while, bam! Faber landed another overhand right and he was in my guard blasting away with his elbows.

My last two fights had been against the bigger and slower Joe Martin and Poppies Martinez. Urijah on the other hand was fast as shit.

The blood drained into my eyes and made it almost impossible to see. Faber stood and I remained on my back. He landed some kicks and then dove on top with a right that landed right on my bloodied forehead.

I struggled for a submission, but I never really had the opportunity. My blood blinded me and Faber continued to bust me up. I tried to retaliate from the bottom and landed a few elbows of my own. They didn't do too much damage though.

The round seemed to drag on for an eternity. My head throbbed and all the damn blood was awful.

Finally, the horn sounded. My corner helped me to my feet and I walked back to the stool on wobbly legs. The doctor looked me over and made the decision. The fight was over.

I had lost for the first time via stoppage. And I felt that it was really the first time I had been beaten up. My belt was gone. Urijah Faber was the new WEC champ, and all I could do was head to the hospital to get my forehead sewed up.

Not a good night at all, and many more bad nights were just around the corner.

Chapter 37

My mom had been adamant right after the Faber fight. "No Pulver. No way!"

That made sense at the time because I was pretty busted up and the fight with Pulver was only six weeks away, but now we were in the amazing Trump Taj Mahal in Atlantic City and I was moments away from stepping into the IFL ring to fight Pulver.

The way I saw it was I had to get back on the horse. I'd been really beaten for the first time and it was either start riding again or hang up my saddle for good. I'd actually gone back and forth on it once again. Fighting wasn't so much fun now. It had become a chase for a bigger payday each time out and I had a hard time reconciling with that.

I'd spent three days pretty much avoiding the reality of a fight. The night before I wondered through the casino floor and made my way to the arena. I was able to slip in and walked to the ring. I stood there in the silence and darkness for a long time. Then I crawled onto the ring and turned onto my back.

It was so peaceful at that moment. I closed my eyes and visualized the fight and thought a lot about my life and my fight career. I eventually drifted off to sleep right there on the canvas.

The following day right before my walkout I peered through the curtain and saw my mom sitting next to Tim Sylvia. He'd just won the UFC heavyweight belt and I think he even had it with him. I walked up behind her and placed my wrapped hands on her shoulders. "I'm retiring after this."

"Good," she replied.

I knew it was what she wanted. She supported me, but the idea of me getting beaten up and bloodied didn't sit well with her. I was still her boy who had run away to protect his friends years earlier, the one she hugged with tears in her eyes and told to never do it again. I was the boy she had fought for at the school in order to keep me from having to constantly fight the kids from the reservation. I was alongside her and my brother during those long and terrible trips to the prison. And she was alongside me when I went to get Gabby.

She didn't like seeing me climb in the cage or ring, even when I won. She wanted me to be safe.

I wasn't completely sure if I believed what I had told her. After all, if I went out there and beat the former UFC lightweight champ I would be riding high once again. And if I lost I didn't know if I could really stomach going out like that.

In any case, I had told her what I thought was the truth and what she needed to hear.

Moments later, I was walking through the curtain once again while sporting my Tapout Underdog Gear shirt with Mike Popp right behind me. He wasn't too fired up about me taking this fight either, but he understood that I needed it.

I climbed through the ropes and waited on Jens Pulver. This fight was back at lightweight, heavier than I wanted, but I now had some experience at it.

The rock music started blaring and Pulver strutted toward the ring. He climbed through the ropes and I had my back to him as Mike rubbed my shoulders. He looked across the ring at Pulver and then quickly said, "Don't look at him."

I followed his instructions, but didn't know why he'd given them.

"When you turn around, just be prepared that he looks huge," Mike added.

When I finally stared across the ring I understood exactly where Mike was coming from. Pulver looked humongous. He had to be at least 170 and he was ripped. I had managed to get all the way up to 153 pounds.

There wasn't time to think about that though. I was in the ring with a guy who had beaten the likes of Caol Uno and B.J. Penn, a guy who weeks earlier had won by KO in Pride. It was an honor to be thought of as a worthy opponent for Jens, but I wanted more than honor. I wanted victory.

We met in the middle of the ring and when we touched gloves Jens smiled. His mouthpiece had shark's teeth on it and it freaked me out. I quickly tried to shake it away.

I fired off a couple hard leg kicks. Jens countered with a left that grazed the top of my head. I landed a short right and Jens countered with a jab. He was fast and strong, but I felt I was quickly settling into the rhythm of the fight.

He threw a hook that flew by me. I could hear it as it missed and I thought, I'm glad that missed.

And then, boom! He caught me with a short left hook. My world tilted a bit and I found myself on my back. Shit! I thought. How could I let that happen? Pulver didn't follow me to the canvas and I rolled back up to my feet.

I circled to my left and found myself against the ropes, and then everything tilted again. It was another left that I never saw coming, and those are the worst. I tried to protect myself, but he landed another big left.

Herb Dean jumped in to stop the fight.

In a matter of six weeks I had been stopped twice. I wasn't sure what to think as I listened to Jimmy Lennon Jr. announce that I had lost to Pulver in just 56 seconds. I clapped as his name was called, and when seeing the replay I noticed that Jens had stopped after just one shot on the ground. I appreciated that and it was just one of the reasons we became such good friends afterward.

Still though, one word ran through my mind as Pulver celebrated...Fuck!

Maybe it really was time to retire? Of course I never could have guessed that in the very near future I wouldn't have a choice in the matter.

Chapter 38

I'd done a lot of thinking on the long flight back to California. I wasn't really ready to quit, but I knew something had to change. I needed to try to reinvent myself. I believed that these two losses could be a learning experience and just a speed bump on the way to the top.

That's why when I got a call from Reed Harris about possibly fighting Eddie Wineland at 135 pounds I decided to take it. There was no way I would fight at 155 again unless it was in the UFC, and at 135 I would be the bigger fighter for a change.

I headed to my mom's house. "I took a fight against Wineland," I said.

"What the hell, Cole? What happened to retiring?"

"I can't do it. I don't think I've really reached my ceiling. Besides, this fight is at 135. It will be a different world."

My mom understood. She knew fighting was in my blood.

It wasn't long after this when I heard the terrible news that Ryan Bennett had been killed in a car wreck. We'd become friends from when he announced my first fights in the WEC and he was a great guy. He loved MMA and worked hard to show it in a positive light. The news hit me, and many others, pretty hard. I knew he had a big family and I thought a lot about his kids and how hard it must be for them.

While training at Pacific Martial Arts, I got another call from Reed. Wineland got injured. He wanted to know if I'd fight Antonio Banuelos instead. I was fine with that.

I hadn't paid much attention to Banuelos' fights because we were at different weight classes, but I knew he was a good fighter. He was best friends with Chuck Liddell and trained with John Hackleman at The Pit.

The fight with Banuelos was just three months after I fought Pulver. I had a lot of weight to cut and it would be my first time dropping to 135. I started training my ass off and cutting calories like crazy. I didn't really know what I was doing and Mike Popp was in Thailand. He'd gone over there to learn knife fighting. He'd be back before my fight, but for the time being I was on my own.

My back was against the wall and this was a win or else scenario in my mind. The only other option would be getting on season five of The Ultimate Fighter, but I knew that the odds of that would be long. It would be much better to put it in my own hands by beating Banuelos.

I continued to cut weight until August 16, 2006, the day before WEC 23. I went to the weigh in and felt completely exhausted. I was sure I had managed to make the 135 weight limit, but as I looked down at the scale I was shocked. I'd dropped all the way down to 132 pounds. I was basically a walking skeleton.

I tried hard to rehydrate and packed on some weight over the next 20 hours, but I still felt like my arms and legs were heavy. No way would I let a little fatigue from my weight cut stop me though.

I met up with Antonio Banuelos and we went back and forth during round one. I just couldn't find my rhythm and struggled through.

Round two was much of the same. After the bell I hauled myself back to my corner and Mike told me that I'd better stop him in the third. He also started rubbing water on my legs and massaging them. It was a trick he'd picked up in Thailand.

Chuck Liddell was working in Banuelos' corner and saw what Mike was doing. He made a scene about it and told the referee that Mike was rubbing something on my legs. Mike explained that it was just water and nothing came of it.

I trudged back out for round three determined to stop Banuelos. I threw some combinations that were a tad off, just missing because my timing was off. I tried for a takedown, but couldn't land it. I kept working, but nothing clicked.

Banuelos hadn't hurt me either and I thought that if I finished strong there might be hope. I did everything I could, and then the final bell sounded.

We stood in the middle of the cage and the winner was announced, Antonio Banuelos by unanimous decision.

That was it. It was like a weight landed on me that shoved me into the ground. I'd lost three in a row and fought like crap in the last one. Maybe I really had reached my ceiling. It was hard to swallow, but maybe I really had achieved all that I could in MMA. If that was the case I didn't need to fight anymore.

I loved the competition. Fighting was in my blood. But after my third loss in 2006 I realized that maybe I needed to hang up my gloves.

Then I got an unexpected phone call that made me reconsider everything.

Chapter 39

I hung up the phone and grabbed a water out of the fridge. I was just back from another long shift at the warehouse. I'd been working there for a couple weeks to make sure I was able to get Gabby what she wanted for Christmas. Moving heavy shit sucked, but my little girl was worth it.

The phone call had my brain spinning. They wanted me to go to Vegas for a possible spot on The Ultimate Fighter season five. I'd taken some much needed time off after the loss to Banuelos and had just trained lightly. I knew TUF was a possibility, but definitely didn't plan on it. I was resigned to taking a break and getting myself both mentally and physically refocused in 2007, but here I was with an amazing opportunity to get on TUF.

The last week of November I found myself locked away in a hotel room in Las Vegas. For the past couple days we'd trained at the UFC gym and I did some interviews with the people running the show.

I was of course excited for the opportunity, but I still wasn't so sure if I was ready to get back after it following the three losses. I'd even left my room to call my mom despite being told not to make any outside calls. I told her that I was considering quitting.

She understood, but she also said that this was such an amazing opportunity. I knew that it really was an incredible opportunity, and decided to stick it out.

The following day I met a young guy from Boston named Joe Lauzon. He was smart and pretty funny and we quickly became friends.

Later in the day we were being shuttled around in the vans that took us back and forth between the hotel and gym. Our driver forgot something and went back inside leaving the keys in the ignition. Joe and I decided this was a great chance for a joy ride and the four or five other guys with us agreed. We figured it would add a little fun to the day and help relieve some of the pressure.

We drove the van around the corner and laughed the whole time. We knew we might be in deep shit, but we found it to be hilarious.

Luckily, Dana White didn't send us home for the stunt. And I also started getting the fire to compete again. It felt like fighting could be fun again.

I stayed there and hung out with Joe for a few more days, and then it was time to head back home. I was unsure if I would actually be on the show or not. They said they'd call soon.

While in Vegas I'd noticed a bump on my arm that looked like a small boil or a pimple. It hurt a little bit, but I didn't think much of it. After returning to Fresno the bump got bigger and it hurt to touch. I showed it to my mom. "You should go see a doctor to get it checked out," she said.

I got an appointment and continued to work at the warehouse and train. It was a fairly tough schedule, but with Christmas right around the corner and a possible spot on TUF 5 I kept at it.

By the time my appointment rolled around the boil had gotten bigger and the skin around it had an odd appearance. Gabby, who was just four years old, sat next to me as the doctor looked at it quizzically and asked me a bunch of questions. I told him that I was a fighter and currently working in a warehouse.

He finally decided that he wanted to cut it and drain it. I agreed, and he made a small incision and squeezed. It hurt like hell and I let out a growling scream as pus bubbled up from the boil. When Gabby saw me in such pain she broke down into tears. I bit my lip and then tried to console Gabs.

I was pissed at the doctor for not warning me that it would hurt so badly. I could have gotten Gabby out of the room so she didn't see her dad in pain.

"What do you think?" I asked the doctor.

He thought it was some kind of infection and gave me some antibiotics. I found it strange that he didn't do anything else, but he was the doctor and he probably knew best.

As I left his office my phone rang. I stopped just outside of the office door and listened closely. Somebody that had been selected for TUF 5 was injured and unable to be on the show. I was in. I would be on season five of The Ultimate Fighter.

Chapter 40

The more I thought about it, the more it sank in. The Ultimate Fighter was the big break I needed. Matt Serra had just won season four and he was slated to fight for the welterweight belt against Georges St. Pierre. If I could go into the house and win the season I might get my own shot at the UFC lightweight title.

Months earlier I decided that I wouldn't fight at lightweight again unless it was in the UFC. Now here I was with the perfect opportunity, however I was well below the 155 pound lightweight limit. It worried me that I'd go into the show way undersized and against really tough opponents like my new friend Joe Lauzon or my old friends Gabe Ruediger and Nate Diaz.

The show's taping was a month away so I started eating like crazy. My mom bought a craploud of Ensure and I downed it like it was water. My weight slowly climbed even as I trained that much harder and continued to work at the warehouse.

After a few days I returned to the doctor. He examined the bump on my arm and thought it was fine and gave me some more basic antibiotics. I thought this was great news because any problem with my body could derail my shot on TUF. Later, I learned that he should have done a culture and cut out a piece of the boil to see what it was, but he didn't do that.

It was around this second visit when my back started hurting. I continued to work at the warehouse even as the pain got worse. I really wanted Gabby to have a great Christmas and my mom had convinced her I was one of Santa's elves. It didn't feel like a muscle strain or tear and I figured it was just general fatigue from training and working.

Two days after it started it had grown to the point where I began to really worry. Christmas was right around the corner and the TUF taping was only a few weeks away. I decided that I had to get back to the doctor.

He checked me out and noted that the boil was almost healed. He also thought that my back was nothing more than muscle pain and gave me some pills for it. He never considered that there could be a link between my past visits and the new back pain. The pills didn't help. Just walking around was miserable, but I sucked it up and finished up at the warehouse.

On Christmas morning I had a hard time wiping the smile off of my face because Gabby was thrilled with her presents, and yet I was overwhelmed with concern because my back was steadily getting worse.

That day I thought about being on the show. Jens Pulver, the guy I had just lost to only eight months earlier, would be coaching against B.J. Penn. I'd become friends with Jens, and B.J. was no doubt one of the best lightweights in the world.

No matter how bad my back was I had to be on that show. I saw it as literally a once in a lifetime opportunity.

Since Christmas was over and TUF was close, I stopped working at the warehouse and gutted through a few more workouts. Finally though, I couldn't take it anymore. It was like somebody was twisting a knife in my lower back. And on top of it I started having a difficult time urinating. Something had to be wrong.

I trekked back to the doctor for a fourth time. I received a cursory check and was told it was muscle and maybe a bladder infection. More pain meds and I was sent on my way.

I made it a couple more days. I'd been experiencing night sweats and gritting my teeth to fight back screams of pain as I tried to sleep. I'd then wake up and struggle through the day in agony. After a short session of excruciating training I made a trip to the emergency room.

They checked me over and gave me some meds for a strained muscle. I couldn't believe it. I was getting absolutely no help and no relief. I disagreed, but I desperately hoped that a strained muscle was the answer. It could heal during the next couple weeks and I may still be able to be on TUF.

I was so close to a shot at the UFC and I now recognized that it was very much in jeopardy.

I couldn't really train because of the twisting knife that I still felt despite the pain meds, and then a few days after the first ER visit I woke up with my legs feeling numb.

Another trip to the ER resulted in zero answers. They gave me more pain meds and pills that were supposed to help me pee, and then they set up an appointment for me to see the urologist.

The TUF taping was now just days away and I sat on the couch in my mom's living room. Cody had driven me over. My mom, who was dealing with her own medical issues with tumors on her pelvis, asked what I thought about TUF. "I've got to get better," I replied.

"Cole, you're not in any condition to compete," she said with a sad look on her face.

"I can recover. Maybe these pills will help." I looked at Cody for support. We had some knock down drag out fights from time to time, but we were still brothers.

He shrugged. "I don't think you can go on the show like this."

I shifted my weight to ease the stabbing in my back. There really was no way I could do it. Deep down I knew it. My huge opportunity was being head kicked by some mysterious fucking back pain.

Later in the day I made a terrible call to Zuffa's (the UFC) office in Las Vegas to let them know I couldn't make it. The call was crushing, but I'd soon learn that it was only the beginning of a march through hell.

Chapter 41

It wouldn't be until later when I would find out that the antibiotics that were supposed to help me were actually killing any good bacteria that might fight my infection. The boil was gone, but a culture was never done so nobody had known what it was.

Now I was back in the ER when I should have been in Las Vegas. I couldn't even think about TUF though. I was more worried about getting through the next few hours. The pain in my back had become debilitating and I still had a terrible time urinating.

I was on a gurney and literally screaming in pain. A nurse on her way to dinner after her shift happened to walk by. She stopped and asked if I'd been seen and asked what was wrong. I tried to explain through gritted teeth.

They thought I had some kind of bladder or kidney or urinary tract infection. She went back to the nurse's station and returned with a shot of morphine for my pain. I would have given her my damn house at that moment if she would have asked for it.

The doctor checked my pain levels. To our complete dismay he decided that I could go home. It wasn't long until my body felt like I was on fire. Later, I'd find out I was allergic to morphine.

Eight hours later and I was back in the hospital. Again, nothing was done except another shot of morphine. This time, when I got out of the hospital bed my legs gave out on me. I crumpled to the floor and it felt like fire ants attacked my lower back.

Cody helped me up and looked at the doctor. "Dude, he can't stand up. You're really going to send him home?"

The doctor responded with some bullshit about the muscle relaxers and blood vessel blockage.

My mom was confused and completely worried. She argued that we had private insurance and pleaded with them to just admit me. No luck.

I got back home and was desperate for sleep. Cody, who was living with me at the time, helped me up the stairs to my room. I just wanted a tiny bit of relief from the absolute agony.

I dropped into my bed exhausted from the constant pain, and fell asleep.

Screaming is what woke me up, and then I realized it was coming from me. My body pulsed with pain and my stomach felt as if it was about to pop. I lifted my head off the pillow and looked down at my stomach. It looked like I'd swallowed a basketball.

This of course freaked me out. I tried to raise myself up and move while still screaming in pain. And then I realized that I couldn't feel or move my legs.

"What's wrong, Cole," Cody yelled as he entered my room.

"I can't move my legs. I can't move them!"

"Oh shit! What should we do?"

"Get me downstairs," I said.

It was then when Cody saw my stomach. "Oh my God, your stomach is huge."

"I know."

He carefully lifted me out of bed and carried me down the stairs. He put me in a chair and called Mom while I moaned in anguish. "Cole can't move his legs. He's paralyzed," Cody said. "Okay, I'll take him to the hospital right now."

We raced through the streets back to the hospital that had done nothing to help me so far. My stomach pulsed with pain and my legs were gone. I was so scared, and for a damn good reason, I feared that if they didn't help me this time I would soon be dead.

Chapter 42

I sat in a wheelchair in the emergency room with my torso feeling as if my guts were about to rip through my skin and dump out on the floor. My legs were now worthless and my head pounded like I'd been beaten with a baseball bat. I moaned and screamed in pain, unable to control myself.

My mom arrived and saw the condition I was in. "He's a cagefighter," she yelled. "If he's like this something is seriously wrong. He's going septic. Get off your asses and do something!"

The staff tried to calm her down, but she was looking at a paralyzed shell of her son in dire need of help. She wasn't calming down one bit. Security came and threatened to make her leave if she didn't settle.

It was about that time when doctors arrived and they wheeled me back into a room. They pumped me full of more morphine, which only hurt like hell. Then they gave me Oxycontin and some other pain medication. I still had no relief.

The doctors ran tests and took blood and did an MRI. Why they couldn't have done all this during one of the previous visits was beyond me, but at the moment I didn't have the energy to be mad. I just wanted to make sure I didn't die and then make sure I could walk once again.

They couldn't figure out what was wrong. It was now the middle of the night and they called a

Dr. Meyer who was supposedly a top-notch neurosurgeon. After talking with him they decided to give me another MRI. I later learned that the first one wasn't of my entire upper body.

I lay in the machine in a drug-induced haze as it clicked and took pictures of my body. It wasn't long after the MRI when they realized that I had a massive epidural abscess in my lower back.

They gave me an IV of a drug to treat Anthrax and it was quickly decided that I would need to see Dr. Meyer immediately and that emergency surgery was most likely the best solution. My head swam with drugs and pain and fear. Everything was spinning out of control. It was like getting rocked in a fight and struggling to recover on wobbly legs, only ten times worse and it lasted much longer.

I heard the sirens of the ambulance as I lay in the back of it, and then I was in a room at the shitty teaching hospital on the wrong side of town. It was the hospital that my mom told me she would never make me go to, but now here I was and it was my only hope.

The next thing I knew I was on a gurney in a hallway in the ER. I had just been wheeled between a guy who was handcuffed to a metal chair and two cops. The doctors told me I needed surgery and started pumping Vancomycin, an antibiotic that is used to treat bacterial infections that don't respond to lesser antibiotics. It's serious shit.

A doctor drew on me and explained that they would go into my spine and try to remove the abscess. They presented a medical authorization. I signed it, desperate for relief despite the very real risks.

My mom arrived and saw that they were prepping me. She flipped out when she saw the markings and the younger doctor looking on. "No way in hell is a medical student doing any surgery on Cole."

Dr. Meyer assured her that it would be only him doing the surgery and he was an expert, but then he explained the risks.

It was so much, so fast. Both my body and brain were twisted up. I wasn't ready for all this, and yet I didn't have a choice. It was like the cage door had been slammed shut and it was time to fight, except this time I didn't have any control over the outcome.

I found myself in a bright room and doctors and nurses buzzed around preparing to cut me open. Then I got feeling in my legs and moved my feet. This created a flurry of activity and a flicker of hope, at least for Cody and my mom and me.

My mom rushed into the room. "You have to retract the authorization, Cole. The antibiotics are working. Don't do the surgery!"

I considered it, but the doctors told me that essentially nothing had changed. "I have to do it Mom. It's my best option."

She couldn't take the rollercoaster of emotions and finally left so they could start sawing away the abscess that had wrapped around my spine.

Dr. Meyer gave me another chance to change my mind. I didn't take it. The drugs to put me to sleep were pumped into my veins. I thought of my life and my fight career. And then I was out.

Chapter 43

As the doctor cut open my back to get to the abscess, I was of course oblivious. I wasn't aware that my red-eyed mom, who had barely slept in the last two days, was pacing in the waiting room or smoking cigarettes outside.

Once she heard epidural abscess she saw my fight career being squashed and she knew that even though I had been struggling with it, fighting meant everything to me. And then she thought of the much worse possibility of me being paralyzed for life. She couldn't stand thinking of me being unable to walk.

I was also unaware that when Jens Pulver heard about my emergency surgery he gathered up a bunch of the guys in the TUF house and said a prayer for me. I was supposed to be there. Instead, I was on an operating table. It was cool to learn that he was thinking of me during such a terrible time.

The doctor and his team got to my spine and were shocked with what they found. A gooey mass had formed around my spine and it was eating through it at an alarming rate. They went to work with the painstaking process of removing the mass without further damaging my fragile spinal cord.

One hour turned to two, and then three and four. The surgery was not supposed to last more than four hours, but the abscess had found its way into every crevice of my spinal column and it had started feasting on my spinal cord.

After almost eight hours of slow and tedious work, the doctor's team stapled me back together. It took 17 staples in all. And then I was finally wheeled into ICU.

It was in ICU when darkness gave way to a foggy light. I didn't know where I was or what I was doing. It felt as if my brain had been scraped clean and the past was lost to me. Then, as the light grew I remembered the insanity of the last two days.

I was in a hospital and I'd had surgery on my back. A nurse arrived and smiled down at me. "There you are. How are you doing?"

"Fine," I managed to croak out from my dry mouth.

"Just relax and rest. You're in recovery."

I tried to nod. I remembered that before the surgery I couldn't feel my legs. I concentrated on my feet and realized that I did have a sense of feeling. Something was different, and that had to be good.

I fell asleep again. When I awoke I felt clearer. The fog was gone and the memories flooded my head. I checked again to see if I could feel my legs. I could, and I was able to move my feet.

The doctor arrived. "How are you feeling, Cole?"

"Okay," I replied.

"It will take some time to recover. We found a lot of damage in your spine. You had something called Methicillin-resistant Staphylococcus aureus."

I looked at him blankly.

"It's better known by its acronym of MRSA. It's basically a flesh-eating bacterium that is very hard to treat. The antibiotics you were taking did not help."

How is it now?" I asked.

"There was extensive damage. I cleaned it out the best I could. Cole, I'm going to be honest with you. You might be able to walk again with a walker, but it's too early to tell."

I nodded my head and took a deep breath. "When can I go back to training?"

The doctor gave me a confused look. "I don't think you understand me. You're not ever going back to training. You're done with that. Let's just focus on walking. Let's see if we can get over that hurdle because it's going to be the biggest."

Nurses started working on me and the doctor squeezed my shoulder reassuringly before leaving. I knew that he had done a great job removing the MRSA abscess. I knew that if it wasn't for him I would be in much worse shape, but at the same time I was lost after hearing what he said.

I stared at the ceiling as the doctor's words slowly settled in. I might not be able to walk again, and if so I will probably use a walker. That thought and all the consequences of it sat on me heavily.

My fight career was over. After the three losses I had toyed with the idea of not fighting. Now though, I desperately wanted the chance to fight again. Giving something up on your own isn't nearly as difficult as when it has been taken away from you. My fight career, something that had defined my adult life and helped me recover from those rough teenage years, was yanked away from me.

Then I thought of my beautiful little girl, Gabby. I thought of how I would not be able to play with her. I would not be able to do so many things that a dad does with his daughter. She loved to dance like little girls do, and I would not dance with her again.

I would be stuck in a stupid wheelchair and sit on the sidelines as she grew up. This thought made a lump grow in my throat and tears form in the corner of my eyes.

I was literally broken.

Chapter 44

This couldn't be real. It was less than a year ago when I was the WEC champ. I was on top of the world and I was strong and healthy. As I stared at the ceiling in the ICU with needles stuck in my body and machines beeping I knew that it was very real, and yet I continued to try to convince myself that this was just some kind of ultra-realistic fucked up nightmare.

Each minute seemed to stretch as I lay in that damn bed. I could feel my legs, but that was little consolation. The doctor's words kept echoing in my head....You're done with training...let's just focus on walking...

The nurses and doctors checked on me frequently and my mom and brother were able to visit for a short time.

It was always a somber affair even though my mom tried her best to remain positive and encouraging. Gabby had come with my mom and Cody a few times. It was so good seeing her, but it was hard. I was her dad, the one who would protect her and care for her, but now I was a shell of the man I had been.

After five days I was cleared to go home. A shiny wheelchair was my ride out of the hospital. Before I was released, the doctor had inserted a PIC line, a catheter that goes directly to the heart. Because of this there was a contraption sticking out of my arm and a line that snaked through my body and ended in my chest. It would be used to administer antibiotics directly to my heart for four hours each day.

We arrived at my house and my brother helped me into a chair. I sat there and looked at the TV blankly. In a matter of days my body had become emaciated and my legs looked and felt so weak.

Day after day went by and I felt like I was in my own purgatory. It was all too much to take and my emotions tumbled between despair and denial and anger.

I went to physical therapy and they had me practice with a walker that they had to strap me into so I wouldn't crash to the floor. I willed my legs to work as they had before, but time after time they just wouldn't respond.

They told me to use the walker whenever I could. I had to shuffle along with it like I was 100 years old. My legs quivered and sometimes they would give out with no warning. I'd have to catch myself with my arms and upper body and then I'd realize just how fucking weak they were as well.

Maybe I should have been elated that I was not completely confined to a wheelchair, but I wasn't. I was still a pathetic heap of bones and muscles.

One afternoon I decided that I had to get out of the house. I asked my mom to take me to Hollywood Video. It was a difficult process, but we finally made it to the video store. I shuffled along at a snail's pace with my mom by my side.

I glanced over and she had a depressed look on her face. "What?" I asked.

"Nothing," she gave me a forced smile.

"What is it, Mom?" I pressed.

"You're just frail looking. It's hard to see you like this." I didn't know how to respond and my mom continued. "You're going to be okay though. I know it."

"I hope so."

We got two movies and headed back home. I sat in the chair and watched them while I drank a beer. This was my life now. I had nothing to offer the world and felt absolutely useless.

After the movies I made my way to the bottom of the stairs. I'd vowed to never be carried up or down them so I lurched my way upward through a combination of holding onto the wall and shuffling and scooting.

As always, by the time I reached the top I was completely exhausted. I made my way to my bed and crumpled into it. As I lay in the darkness I wondered if I would ever have anything to offer anybody again.

I seriously doubted it.

Chapter 45

The clock seemed to morph into my ugly tormenter as hours upon hours ticked by with me sitting in my house doing absolutely nothing. I was so depressed and my body was so broken. I was weak and pathetic and no matter what I did my legs wouldn't work right. The nerve impulses from my brain just couldn't reach my legs efficiently. It was like water trying to get through a hose that had a bunch of kinks in it.

I'd totally given up on the idea of ever training again, let alone fighting. It was so hard to reconcile with this thought. I'd been healthy and strong for a long time and it was hard to wrap my head around the fact that I was now broken.

One afternoon I was sitting on my couch with the IV pumping the high-powered antibiotics into my heart when the doorbell rang. I hated having the PIC catheter jammed in me. It was a constant reminder of how bad off I was.

My mom, who was there to help me around the house, asked who was at the door. "The guys from the casino," I replied.

Through the last few years of fighting I'd become friends with some of the casino owners and they'd called to tell me they were getting me out of the house.

A moment later the living room was filled with a handful of my friends. It was good to see them, and yet I didn't want them there. They asked me a bunch of questions and then one of them said, "Come on bro, get your ass ready."

"I can't go anywhere right now. Look at me."

"Bullshit, you need to get out. We're taking you to the casino."

The idea of sitting at a Blackjack or Poker table was a lot more appealing than daytime TV, so I slowly got myself ready while the antibiotics continued to pump into my heart.

The IV bag was almost empty by the time I shuffled between the slot machines and tables with the aid of my walker. My friend helped by rolling the metal tree that held the IV bag and I eventually worked myself into a stool at a two dollar Blackjack table.

The waitress came by as I was unhooking the IV. She looked at me with pity and my face flashed hot with a mix of anger and embarrassment. "Don't worry, I'm fine," I said. "I'll take a beer please."

She gave me a sideways look. "A beer?"

"Yeah, a beer."

She shrugged her shoulders and walked away, returning a few minutes later with my drink. I gave her a dollar tip and took a long drink. This was the beginning of a four-week bender.

I was so depressed and beaten. I'd had 15 fights and an 11-4 record. I'd lost to Bao Quach, Urijah Faber, Jens Pulver and Antonio Banuelos. They'd beaten me in the cage and that sucked, but now this fucking MRSA had beaten my spirit, and it was infinitely worse. Drinking the frustration away seemed to be a good solution.

My venue eventually shifted from the casino to a local sports bar. Every day my friends picked me up and took me there. By noon I'd be well on my way to drowning my reality in booze. I figured that I couldn't break myself any more than I already was so I might as well dull it all by getting drunk.

After a week my mom started getting worried. After two weeks she was real worried and she told me so. I blew her off and continued my downward spiral. During the third week she berated me, told me that I was being a quitter and that I wasn't being a good dad to Gabby. The words stung, but not enough. I was back at the bar later that day.

My life was over. I was just 25 years old and I shuffled along with a walker. I'd been able to fight against the best guys in the world and now I was reduced to a sad heap that the waitresses looked at with pity.

I had accepted this new weak version of myself as the best I would ever be. Words like walker, crippled, broken, retired, had become the standard definition of me. My life was basically over and I had come to accept this new existence.

After about a month of being sad and pathetic and getting shitfaced every day I started wondering how long I would continue to do this. Was there an end in sight or would I keep self-destructing?

I'd just gone to take a piss and returned to the bar. I still used my walker and leaned on it to pull myself back up on the barstool. By the time I was perched on my stool beads of sweat had formed on my forehead. I wiped them away and was ordering a beer when my mom showed up beside me.

"Cole, I've had enough of this shit. You need to lead, follow, or get the fuck out of the way! I'm not doing this anymore. You need to make a decision."

She then turned and walked away. I thought I was doing a pretty good job of getting the fuck out of the way, but I'd also been thinking about how I was being unfair to the people who loved me the most. I hadn't spent near as much time with Gabby. It was so hard for me to have her see me in my current condition.

I also started thinking about others who had been through terrible situations. I remembered my friend, Ryan Bennett, and thought of how hard it must be for his kids after he passed away in the car wreck. I wondered how they were coping with losing their dad, and then I thought about how Gabby was doing. She'd essentially lost me over the last two months.

I drank my beer and contemplated about it all. I'd been to the doctors and physical therapists and they told me that now they believed I could walk without assistance once again, but I'd still never be able to fight. I'd have to live with that and find peace with it for the sake of my daughter.

Chapter 46

My PIC line was removed and it felt like I'd earned a little bit of freedom. I was slowly gaining strength and had grown to realize that I could still have a decent life. I remembered what the doctor said about focusing on walking and that it would be the biggest hurdle.

As I was beginning to come out of my depression I got a call from Christian Printup. We had been friends, but then had our differences stemming from the Poppies Martinez fight and became friends again. He wanted to see me so I got a ride to The Palace and hobbled through the casino with my walker.

When Christian saw this frail version of me he almost started crying. He knew how hard this was for me as a man. He gave me a hug and we talked for a bit.

"Listen, I asked you to come down because when I heard what happened I talked to the tribal council. You've done a lot for all of us through the years with your commitment and putting on great fights. We know that you can't work now so we decided we wanted to give you something to help out and show our appreciation."

Christian handed me a piece of paper. I looked down at it. It was a check for five thousand dollars. I felt a rush of emotions and looked up at Christian. "I don't know what to say."

"It's not a lot. I wish we could give you more."

"It is too a lot." I gave him a hug. "I can't tell you how much this means to me."

The money was definitely needed, but it was more than just a monetary thing. The gesture showed me that I still had some value as a person, not just as a fighter. Of course I knew my family loved and appreciated me, but with this coming from Christian and the tribe it really hit home.

After leaving the casino I determined that if I could walk on my own then I could focus on the next hurdle. Deep down in the depths of my soul I think there was a tiny spark that still yearned for the cage, but when I'd take a step on shaky legs it was like the spark was doused with water.

Just focus on walking. That was my hurdle. Finally, I decided that I would not use the walker again. I wasn't completely ready, but I didn't care. "I'm done with the walker," I told my mom while sitting at the kitchen table.

"Good," she replied. "I've got something for you for when you're ready."

She plucked an envelope off of the counter and slid it in front of me. I ripped it open and looked inside. It was coupons for driving a NASCAR and skydiving. I looked at them and my pulse sped up a bit. The thought of doing both was exhilarating. But then a wave of sadness sank over me.

"I can't do these things," I said.

"Not now, but one day you'll be able to do them."

She walked out of the kitchen before I could respond. I sat there and thought about it. Maybe she was right. Maybe one day I could do them.

Over the next few weeks I struggled to walk on my own. I often had to use the wall or a table to keep from falling, but I didn't use the walker. My legs hurt so damn bad, but I kept moving forward one tiny step at a time. And eventually I gained a little more confidence and felt better about myself.

I had been unable to make myself go back to the gym. I didn't want all the guys to see me like I was. I didn't want them to look at me with pity like the waitresses at the sports bar and so many others had done. Those people were strangers and their looks of pity still hurt. I had a hard time imagining how I would respond when my friends, the guys I had fought side by side with, looked at me with pity.

Now though, as I continued to gain strength in my legs while visualizing racing around a track or jumping out of a plane, I decided that I needed to go to the gym. The walking hurdle was being climbed and that spark for the cage flickered. Maybe the NASCAR and skydiving would be just the beginning.

It was a bright Saturday morning, the kind where people are out and about and in a good mood and you have to squint if you aren't wearing sunglasses. I was in a good mood as well, a better mood than I'd been in in a long time.

The parking lot of Pacific Martial Arts was nearly full for the Muay Thai smoker. It had been so long since I'd been back to the gym and a nervous excitement coursed through my veins. I did worry about how everybody would react to this broken down me who looked like he had Parkinson's when he walked, but I thought I was ready for it.

As I got out of the car I got the instant urge to go to the restroom. One of the side effects of my surgery was that my bladder and bowels were weak. When I needed to go I had to go right away. There was no holding it. My stomach started turning and I realized that I was in dire need of the toilet.

I shuffled along on shaky legs toward the front door. I swung it open and lurched forward toward the restroom. The gym was packed and a lot of eyes were turned toward me. And that's when it happened. I couldn't hold it any longer and the toilet was too far away.

Right there in the gym I shit myself.

I was unsure if people could tell or not. Some were trying to talk to me or were approaching me as it happened. I muttered that I had to go and turned and made my way for the door. My fucking broken body had betrayed me again. It was the most embarrassed I had ever been, and as I headed back home I vowed that I would not return to the gym. How could I? I couldn't even keep from pissing or shitting on myself.

The gym was no place for someone like me.

Chapter 47

After the gym incident I didn't want to do a damn thing. The flicker in my soul had been snuffed out and I just tried to get through each day. I was walking, but in order to propel myself forward my whole body would shake and I was still holding onto the wall from time to time for support.

I'd started gaining some weight and my bladder and bowels had gotten a little stronger. I still couldn't hold it in for very long so on the few occasions when I did leave the house I made sure I was always close to a restroom.

My mom decided that she wanted to get me some new clothes so we headed to the mall. As we arrived she said. "So how about the NASCAR deal, are you close to trying it?"

I knew she was trying to pull me out of my funk with the clothes and now mentioning the long forgotten NASCAR coupon. I'd shoved it onto a shelf in my room along with the skydiving coupon. "I don't know if I'm ready for that," I replied.

"Sometimes you don't have to be ready to try something new."

She was right, but she also wasn't a shambling zombie when she walked. I thought about it as we shopped, but my legs grew weaker and weaker as the day wore on and it became harder to walk. We were almost finished when I took a step and my legs stopped working.

I dropped onto the floor like I'd been knocked out. I was angry and ashamed at the same time, and I refused my brother's help as I pulled myself back up to a standing position.

"Let's go home," I said.

After the mall trip I again went back to sitting around and watching TV or surfing the web. I felt so sorry for myself as one day bled into another. I'd reconciled with the idea of never fighting again, now I just wanted a normal life. I wanted to walk without fear of falling and go places without fear of crapping myself. I wanted to play with my daughter and take her to the park. But none of that was really happening.

Gabby and I spent time together around the house and we watched Disney movies, but I was so limited, both physically and emotionally. My world had been dulled and darkened around the edges and it stayed that way for a long time.

"You've got to get some adrenaline pumping through your veins again," my mom finally told me. "Go do the NASCAR deal."

I eventually relented just to get her off my back, and the day finally came for me to climb behind the wheel of a NASCAR and fly around the racetrack. That morning I had second thoughts, but forced myself to go. I'm glad I did. It was completely badass and as I drove over a hundred miles per hour I forgot about my busted legs.

The exhilaration pushed away a little bit of the dullness and I decided that maybe it was time to visit the gym once again. The last time was burned into my brain and I doubted the feelings of shame would ever fully go away, but something deep down pushed me to take another shot at the gym. There was an upcoming Jiu Jitsu tournament and the more I thought about it the more I looked forward to it.

This time I made it through the door without any incident and a few of my training partners tried to make small talk. It was weird though. My friends had a hard time looking at me. It was like a gray cloud of depression hung over me and pulled the others into it.

I was the former champ. I was the guy who had kicked ass and taken names. I'd been in the cage with some of the best fighters in the world and now I was reduced to a guy who used the wall for support and shook like a naked kid standing in the snow when I walked.

The others didn't want me to see them looking at me with pity and sadness so they resorted to quick glances and clipped words. I couldn't blame them. I was a cautionary tale, a horrible reminder of their fragility and even mortality.

I made it through the hard day, but because of it I decided that I really had to be done with the gym. I loved it so much and I loved the guys there, but it wasn't fair to them or me to be up there.

Again, I returned to my cave where I struggled along to come to grips with my new life. I did eventually do the skydiving. It was a nice shot of much needed adrenaline that helped me feel more alive, and yet there was still this weird hole in me that sucked the life out of me.

Chapter 48

It wasn't long after the skydiving that Randy Harris of Talking Sports Radio was putting together an auction for Ryan Bennett's family. I thought about Ryan and his kids and I thought about my own life. I was still broken down, but at least I could be here for Gabby.

I also thought about the generosity of Christian and the tribe and how much I appreciated it. The idea of auctioning something to help Ryan's kids really hit home. I wanted to help out, but I couldn't figure out what to auction. Then I had an idea. "I've been thinking about what to do for Ryan's kids," I said to my mom. "I'm thinking about auctioning my WEC belt."

It meant so much to me, but the idea of helping meant a lot more. A wry smile spread across her face. "Good, then I guess you'll have to go get another belt won't you?"

Another MMA title seemed oceans away from where I was now, but I also felt that spark within me once again. "Yeah, maybe so," I replied.

I signed the belt and then wrote 'For Ryan, my friend.'

Over the coming weeks I focused harder on repairing my body and getting stronger. I still couldn't stomach the idea of going back to Pacific Martial Arts even though I knew that if there really was any hope of me ever fighting again I'd have to start training.

Then I learned that a new gym, LA Boxing, was looking for an MMA instructor. I wrestled with the idea for a little bit. I had to do something more than I was doing. My life had been in a terrible holding pattern that was full of turbulence. I had to move forward.

A different gym might be a better way to ease back into it. Besides, it would be a shame to waste my experience and knowledge. I could at least teach others what I had learned even if I'd never apply my knowledge in the cage again.

I took the job and made my way to my new gym. It was a small building with palm trees dotting its landscape. Inside there was a ring and some floor space and a handful of heavy bags. Not much, but I was nervous on my first day.

This was such a huge step for me and I'd just kind of taken it. I hadn't consulted anybody or spent a lot of time weighing my options. I took this as a positive sign because it meant I was ready for it. Or at least I hoped that was the case.

I started teaching Jiu Jitsu classes. I wasn't very hands on. I'd explain the basics and have my students drill. Every now and then I'd get on the floor with them and show them technique, but mostly I explained. I just didn't fully trust my body. It had betrayed me so often over the last year and it was still weak.

As the weeks went by I slowly found myself on the mat more and more. Soon I was showing instead of explaining and my body was responding okay. My legs still shook and I was still weak, but I was back on the mat and it was like I was being rebuilt piece by piece.

Pro fighter Mike Martinez had even started training some with me and I had a couple other higher level students. I started actually rolling with them and my mom's comment about getting a new belt crept into my thoughts from time to time.

The idea remained so far out there, but each time I got on the mat it seemed like I was swimming towards it. I still dealt with terrible leg pain if I pushed too hard, and sometimes I still lost control of my legs, but not as often.

On my routine visit to the doctor I told him what I was doing. He shook his head in amazement and told me that based on the damage to my spine it was almost a miracle that I was even able to walk. I told him about the loss of leg control and the shakiness.

"That's just going to be one of the lingering effects you're going to have from the trauma of the infection being on your spine. It's just one of the side effects you're going to be left with," he said.

I'd just have to learn to cope and I was fine with that. He told me that I was at a higher risk for spinal damage, but despite the concern of becoming permanently paralyzed I was determined to try to actually come back no matter how many more setbacks I'd have to endure.

Chapter 49

After working with Mike Martinez for a month or so I got a call from Popppies. We weren't exactly best friends after we fought a few years earlier so I was surprised and glad to hear from him. He wanted me to help corner him for his upcoming fight.

I was cool with that because it would get me that much closer to the excitement of the cage. I really liked working with Mike and this would also give me a chance to talk with Christian Printup. He was running Palace Fighting Championships and he'd been an integral part of helping me dig out of my despair.

I kicked up my training a notch and started really pushing myself on the mat. My back and legs got horribly sore and my legs quivered even more than usual because of the harder workouts. Sometimes if I worked them too hard they would simply not move right for the rest of the day and I'd have to go lie down and take it easy. Then they'd be sore for days to come like I'd been climbing a mountain.

Despite the pain, I knew that now that I was getting further invested into really trying to make a comeback I'd have to push myself as much as possible. Some days I felt pretty good. Other days completely sucked and I'd look at my quivering legs and think that I was chasing an impossible dream.

On the day of Poppies' fight I got to the casino really early and tracked down Christian. It had been a while since we'd seen each other and we spent a minute catching up. Then I got down to why I came. "I'm coming back and I want a fight when I'm ready."

Christian gave me an "are you BS'ing me" look.

"I'm serious. Can you give me a fight when I'm ready?"

To my surprise, Christian agreed. I left his office and made my way through the casino. My legs were so tired from all the training and as I turned a corner around a slot machine they started to give out. I stumbled into a slot machine and the old lady who was sitting in front of it glared up at me.

"Sorry," I mumbled, and then gathered myself and walked away on my shaky legs. After only a few steps I stumbled again.

Dammit, I thought. My legs HAVE to get stronger. And then a security guy stepped in front of me. "Had too much to drink?" He asked smugly.

"Nothing at all."

He stepped toward me and started to speak again when Christian happened to walk by. He asked what was going on. "He's drunk," the guard said.

"No he's not. Let him go," Christian replied.

Later on, I learned that after this little incident Christian felt terrible for me. He knew that I desperately wanted to fight again, but that it would be a miracle for me to ever get back in the cage.

I was still thinking about what happened in the casino a few hours later as I stood cage side for Poppies' fight. It was such an adrenaline rush to be back near the cage and in the mix. I was so glad he'd asked me to corner him. The crowd, the fights, the excitement, it all got my heart pumping and I was pinging with energy.

Then during Poppies' fights I managed to kick the spit bucket across the floor. People looked at me like I was crazy. I didn't do it on purpose, my damn leg just involuntarily jerked and the bucket happened to be in the way.

It was kind of embarrassing, and coupled with the security guard incident I started wondering if the idea of fighting again was a complete fairy tale. Maybe rolling on the mats and coaching was where I needed to be.

Then I thought of the doctors and how they had given me almost no hope. I had to try my best to comeback simply to prove that I could do it. I had to show that there was always hope no matter how bleak the situation seems.

I went back to LA Boxing and continued to teach and train as much as my body would allow. I continued to push myself even when my legs burned and shook and my back throbbed with pain. I'd become fully invested in the idea of fighting once again, and then I heard that my old gym was having a smoker in the not too distant future.

It was time to test myself.

Chapter 50

There were about 150 people crammed into the gym for the smoker. It was an exciting atmosphere because fighters with varying experience and skill levels were getting their chance to get a taste of real competition. It was their chance to test themselves. I knew this more than anybody else because I was about to go through a huge test, one that would tell me how far I had come and how far I still had to go.

It had been about 16 months since I'd had the emergency surgery. The road from the surgery to this point had been long and twisting and full of potholes. I'd already defied the doctors by just being able to walk, but I wanted more than that so badly.

I stood in the ring with my hands wrapped and looked across at my opponent. I then looked to my right and saw my mom. She was about as worried as I had ever seen her.

It had taken a ton of persuading to talk Mike Popp into letting me fight in the smoker. He wanted to get assurance from my doctor that it was safe. Of course, the doctor couldn't say that it was one hundred percent safe because my spine was still damaged after the infection. It was impossible to be certain that I'd be okay to fight.

Despite the lack of assurance, I finally managed to get Mike to give me a chance at it. Then we had to find somebody willing to fight me.

Nobody was exactly fired up about the idea. I'd like to think it was because I was a former champ, but I'm pretty sure it was because nobody wanted to be the one to beat up the crippled kid.

Finally, a young guy stepped up and said he'd do it. Now, I stared across at him and wondered what was going on in his head. I shook my legs out and hoped that they would work like they were supposed to, and then it was time.

We tapped gloves and started fighting. I tried to fire off punches and kicks and did my best to roll when we hit the mat, but I was a step slow at every turn. My body, and more specifically my legs, just wouldn't react as they should.

After round one my legs were heavy and I was breathing out of my mouth. After round two my legs were heavy and shaky and my arms felt like noodles. After round three I was completely exhausted. I was so tired and my legs just totally shut down. I couldn't even walk out of the ring. Mike Popp had to literally carry me out. I looked around at the faces in the gym. They tried to be encouraging, but I could see it in their eyes that they felt bad for me.

I'd done everything I could. I'd put it all out there and fought with every ounce of myself and I'd gotten a harsh dose of reality. I wasn't even close to ready. The road back to the cage would be much longer than I'd thought.

Over the next week I couldn't do much of anything. My body was too spent and my mind was numb from the experience.

It could go one of two ways. I could go back to the safety of coaching and teaching or I could dig even deeper, find something within me that I'd never found before and do everything that I could to make it.

The first was much more appealing in the short term, but the second idea was the only way I could feed my warrior spirit. As I lay on the couch willing my body to recover from the smoker I made the decision that I was all in, no matter what.

Chapter 51

Sometimes you make a decision that you just absolutely know is right. Deep down you feel that it is a foregone conclusion. That's how I felt after the smoker. Once I was able to get back to training I knew that I was marching toward a date in the distant future that would see me back in the cage.

I also knew that the time between now and then would be long and hard, but I didn't care. I'd been through so many ups and downs, and even though I still had a long ways to go, I had come so far. In my mind and my heart there was no turning back. I was on a mission to show myself, the doctors and everybody else that no matter how desperate the situation seems there is always hope.

I started training twice a day with everything I had. I busted my ass in the gym in the morning. I conditioned on my shaky weak legs after my morning session. I trained in the late afternoon despite the pain and fatigue. I even trained on my own late at night sometimes.

One month after another went by and I remained focused. The summer of 2008 gave way to the fall, and word was getting out that I was almost ready to make a comeback.

Mike Popp had been with me every step of the way and pushed me hard. After an afternoon conditioning session he mentioned that he thought it might be a good idea to look into getting me a fight.

"You think I'm ready?"

"If you want to do it, I know you're ready."

"Yeah, I want it."

It was such a big moment. I'd gone after this seemingly impossible comeback because I had to be the one to make the decision about my future, not doctors or anybody else.

Christian Printup got a fight lined up for me in late 2008. I was worried about how my body would respond, but I was ready. Then the fight was canceled.

It was a brief letdown, but Christian came back with another offer. He asked if I'd want to fight a young kid named Michael McDonald. He'd started his career after I had been decimated with the staph infection. As I struggled to learn to walk again, Mikey had been blasting through one opponent after another. He was 7-0 with seven dominating first-round finishes.

He had to be about the worst opponent possible for a comeback fight, but I didn't care. I wanted it and I was ready, or so I thought.

With news of the fight I started getting a lot of interview requests. Of course everybody wanted to know about the staph infection and my recovery. I made it a point to talk about it as much as I could, even as it got boring and repetitive.

I did so because I recognized that it was opening people's eyes to the dangers of staph. Before my ordeal we didn't know much about it. It's everywhere, and yet we didn't really think about it.

In a weird way it's like I was lucky in a sense for getting sick simply because I was well-known fighter. Everybody took notice and it gave me an opportunity to build awareness in the combat sports and wrestling community.

As I told my story, more and more articles popped up…What is Staph…How do I know if I have Staph…How do I clean my gym to avoid Staph…What do I do if I get Staph… Nobody had talked about it before, and now it was this huge thing. So as I prepared for Michael McDonald I continually talked about my staph infection and the horrible problems it caused.

Now there are companies whose product line is geared toward preventing staph and other dangerous infections.

During all those interviews I thought back to the time we went on the Jenny Jones show. Back then I was angry with my mom for dragging me to Chicago and laying our personal lives out for the world to see, but I now realized exactly why she did it.

If I could be paralyzed and get back into fighting and show people that if you want something bad enough, you can do it, then all the talking was worth it. Even if it motivated just one person in a similar position as mine to get up out of the chair and do something, or if it motivated gyms to strive to keep their members safe, it was fine with me.

If all the suffering and pain and struggle helped one kid do something better or something he thought he couldn't, then I was all for it. Sure, I didn't like having to go through all of it for the outcome, but when my story inspired others it made it seem worth it.

It became personal to me, but I also had a fight to prepare for. And despite my training and my desire to climb back in the cage, there was no way to truly simulate an all-out fight with a hungry kid who was crushing his opponents. My back might not be as strong as I thought, or my legs might start to go funky on me. The only way to find out was to climb in the cage, and May 8th of 2009 was fast approaching.

Chapter 52

Usually right before a big fight, like after I'd entered the cage, I'd have a sense of calm. I'd guess it is that way with a lot of guys. You've busted your butt for so long and have done every possible thing you can to prepare. When you stand in the cage with your opponent the long and tedious preparation process is over. Now you get to show the results of all that hard work.

As I stared across the ring at Michael McDonald I didn't really have that sense of calm. I'd trained so hard. I'd done everything possible and felt that I was actually in better shape than I'd ever been before, but my nerves pinged with apprehension.

There is just no way to simulate a real fight. My back had held up well during hard training and heavy sparring, but as I looked at Michael McDonald and waited for the bell to ring I was entering into a new world. Or at least it was a new me in an old world I'd once known.

I thought that my back would be fine and that I would fight as I did before the surgery. But as I stood there my head was filled with uncertainty. I remembered those horrible nights leading up to the emergency surgery and how broken my body was. I remembered the doctors telling me I may not ever walk again and that fighting was out of the question. I remembered those terrible days of despair when the PIC line pumped antibiotics into my heart and I shuffled along with my walker. I remembered the smoker and how I thought I was ready back then.

I'd come so far. Some said it was a one in a million shot, and yet here I was. Was I really ready? Was my back really capable of taking the stress of a fight? Would I be able to withstand the viciousness that this kid had been unleashing on his opponents?

The referee asked if I was ready and all the memories and concern vanished. It was time to do what I knew best, fight.

McDonald came out fast. He had that look of invulnerability in his eyes. It made sense because he hadn't felt what it was like to be on the losing end yet. The fight seemed to be at Mach speed.

I reminded myself that I had been here many times. I tried to relax and breathe and settle into the fight. I started to feel good and got into the rhythm. We hit the canvas and I gained the mount. I rained down punches and elbows and saw an opening for an armbar. I spun and straightened his right arm.

The round was almost over and I cranked hard. I felt a tap and the bell sounded. I thought I'd won, but the referee didn't see the tap.

My body was responding well and any ring rust from the long forced layoff was being shaken away. Between rounds I was winded, but felt good. In round two I continually got the best of Mike. I took his back and looked for a rear naked choke, but couldn't finish. I then got top control and took the mount. Again I landed punch after punch. Mike struggled underneath me for a long time, but with each punch I felt a little of the fight leaving him.

Finally, about halfway through the second round the referee dove in to stop it.

I stood and raised my hands toward the sky. I was filled with a flood of emotions and an enormous sense of relief sank over me. I was back. I'd been given no chance, and yet here I was with my arms raised in victory.

Chapter 53

I'd just finished helping Gabby with some homework and was on another interview. The guy was of course asking me about my fight and how it felt to win. I told him that it was a huge relief because I wasn't sure how my back would hold up and I knew that Mike McDonald would be a tough opponent.

He then asked more questions about the long and difficult comeback road and I told him that what it came down to was having a support system. I'd been so fortunate to have a great team that believed in me and tremendous coaches. And then I had an amazingly supportive family that stayed with me every step of the way.

When I thought back I recognized that I'd always had some form of a support system. Even when my dad was arrested and went away, his brothers became a bigger part of my life and helped me out. And then after I figured out that my mom's friend, Steve, wasn't going to kill me, he too became a positive force in my life.

It had been a crazy ride since way back when I was a kid, and my return to the ring was no different. In spite of the past struggles I started setting my sights on the next goal. I'd wanted to return to the WEC to reclaim my belt since I started getting the idea of a comeback in my mind. Now though, there were beginning to be a few rumblings that the UFC was considering adding weight classes below lightweight.

I thought back to the TUF tryout just before I got the bump on my arm that lead to my walk through hell. The idea of actually making it in the UFC started digging itself into my brain. I'd just won a huge comeback fight, but I was hungry for more. That's why when I got a call to fight a guy named Tyler Weathers with only a six week recovery period since the McDonald fight, I jumped at it.

I continued to train my ass off and spent hours on end in the upstairs gym in blistering heat. Unfortunately, only a week or two before the fight I started coughing and my lungs felt like they were full of fluid.

There was no way I'd let a cold stop me, and I made a trip to the doctor to see if he could give me something to hold it off until after the fight. He shook his head with concern. "You've got bronchitis. I wouldn't recommend fighting."

I decided not to tell Popp or anybody else, not even my mom, about the doctor's prognosis. I was too hungry and I didn't want another setback during my career rebirth.

As I warmed up, I already felt exhausted, but tried hard not to show it.

My mom wondered if I was alright. I told her I was. When the fight started it was obvious that I wasn't good. I struggled through each round as if I was fighting in sand. Nothing was sharp and I felt dizzy and weak as I gasped for each breathe and gulped air between rounds.

We went to the cards and I squeaked it out with a split decision.

Afterward, my mom and Mike and I were backstage.

"What's wrong with you, Cole?" My mom asked.

"I have bronchitis."

"Are you kidding me?" She turned to Mike. "How could you let him fight this way?"

He shrugged and raised his palms toward the sky. "I didn't know he was this sick."

"It's true," I added. "I didn't tell anybody."

"Why not?"

"I didn't want to have to drop out. I'm back and I want to fight."

Neither one of them were happy with me for not telling them, but they also realized that you just can't really fuck with total determination, and that was what I had now.

Chapter 54

I paced back and forth and shook my arms as I listened to Jimmy Lennon Jr. announce Jeff Bedard. He looked like a tank at only five foot five. Jimmy talked about Jeff being an Olympic caliber wrestler. I didn't need the reminder.

Once again, I was in the Tachi Palace, this time for Tachi Palace Fights 3 and a shot at the bantamweight belt. I'd been here so many times, and had both bad and good memories. My most recent memory of the Palace was when I'd made my triumphant return by beating Mikey McDonald. He'd fought earlier in the evening and surprised many people by putting a beating on Manny Tapia.

After just getting by Tyler Weathers and recovering from the bronchitis, I fought in Strikeforce and TKO'd Maurice Eazel with a head kick and punches. Since then, I'd been training my ass off to prepare for Jeff Bedard. I had total respect for him as an opponent and knew the he was a wrestling machine.

Jimmy Lennon Jr. turned to me and started talking. I continued to pace back and forth. I was relaxed and confident. My back still hurt from time to time and my legs got shaky after hard workouts, but I'd now tested myself completely. My spine was so damaged that I had a higher risk of injury than other fighters, but I decided that it was worth the risk.

With each fight and victory I felt that I was further demonstrating to the world that there was always hope. If I'd listened to the doctors I'd still be hobbling around with a walker or pushing myself in a wheelchair.

Jimmy finished my introduction and the hometown crowd cheered loudly. It was time to test myself again.

We met in the middle of the cage and touched gloves. We each threw a few punches to get into the fight. We clinched briefly and all a sudden I was on my back. Jeff took me down with ease, but I expected the fight would take place on the ground. It was now his wrestling against my jiu jitsu.

He tried to rough me up from the top, but he wasn't landing much. He worked us toward the fence. The fence was a good place for him because it made it harder for me to move and look for a submission, or at least that's what was thought.

My shoulders and head were crammed against the fence. Jeff tried to get separation so he could punch me. I struggled to control his head so I wouldn't get punched. He finally gained a little separation by punching my ribs and pushing to his feet.

Once this happened I realized that the fence was my friend. I was able to push off of it with my shoulders and suck my hips further underneath him. This gave me the opportunity to throw my legs up and work for a triangle.

I cinched it in and squeezed. I knew Jeff had prepared for hours on end against my ground game and I didn't really expect that I could land a triangle, but here I was just moments away from him tapping. He was on his feet so I used my right hand to reach out and pull the back of his left knee. He collapsed and I locked the triangle in even tighter. Ten seconds after landing it, I felt Jeff tap.

I jumped up and spread my arms and ran across the cage to celebrate. I'd given up my belt so long ago to help Ryan Bennett's family, and it was then that I first voiced the idea of actually getting another belt. Of course at the time I was barely able to walk and had to worry about shitting myself.

Now, I was climbing the fence in celebration and pointing to the cheering crowd. I was a champion again, but I still wanted more!

Chapter 55

The small van turned off the busy street into a narrow alley that spilled into another alley. After a little bit it made a right down yet another alley, and then a left. I was somewhere in the eastern part of Tokyo. It had been an incredible ten days since I got a call to fight at Dream 13 against Yoshiro Maeda.

I'd never been out of the United States before and had always wanted to visit Japan, now I was here and getting paid for it. Of course that was if I made it to the fight. As the Japanese guy pulled open the van door I was thinking that this was not where I was supposed to be.

A couple hours earlier I'd asked about a sauna. The ones by the hotel would not take me because of my tattoos. They associated them with gangsters. We piled into a van so they could take me to a different sauna. As we drove I marveled at how clean and orderly the streets were and stared at the buildings. People were everywhere and it was such a unique scene for me.

Then we entered the maze of alleyways.

I started getting uneasy and tried to explain to the guy that I needed a sauna.

"Hai," he replied.

He came to a stop and pulled open the door. I stared at a small building.

"This is the sauna?"

"Hai."

I climbed out and headed inside, sure that I was about to be mugged and killed.

Now I was in a bath house in my sweats and hoodie trying to sweat out the last few pounds. The naked Japanese guys looked at me like I was crazy. And all I could think about was the movie, Eastern Promises, where he has to fight naked in a sauna. I envisioned myself throwing down with some Yakuza when I was supposed to be cutting weight

The sauna went off without an Eastern Promises scene playing out, but it was so damn hot that it melted my water bottle.

I made it back to the hotel in plenty of time for my pre-fight interview, but I was still a couple pounds over. I ended up turning my hotel bathroom into a sauna with the scalding hot water and dropped the final couple pounds. During the interview I sat at a table and listened to the reporters asked their questions in Japanese and then waited for my translator to give me the English version.

I talked about my Samurai spirit and how either you are born with it or not. I told them that I was born with it. If not, I wouldn't be where I was. I mentioned my difficult upbringing without my father and then I talked of my staph infection and surgery.

The Japanese reporters were interested in this, and I realized that they didn't really know about all that I had been through. They asked a bunch of questions about it and I explained what had happened once again.

After the interview I stayed around the hotel and tried to relax. It was such a surreal experience to be in Japan and preparing to have a huge fight against a really tough opponent. Maeda was 26-7-2 coming into the fight and he'd been in with some very tough guys. Once I took the fight I went back and watched his fights with Charlie Valencia and Miguel Torres. He was really good and I knew I'd have my hands full, but I was prepared. It had been just six weeks earlier when I beat Bedard, and I didn't really get out of shape afterward. However, over the last week and a half I kicked my training into overdrive to prepare for Dream's ten-minute first round.

As I waited for the fight I thought about what I'd told the reporters regarding my tough upbringing and my Samurai spirit. I also thought about the infection and the surgery. Despite it being a terrible ordeal, it had made me a better fighter and even a better person.

Before it happened I took things for granted. I got by more on talent and less on hard training and a desire to learn. I'd truly lost what I didn't even really know I had. It took the long climb out of the hole to really recognize this.

The night before the fight I walked along the busy streets. I thought back to the interview and how I was asked what fighting meant to me. "I don't really like fighting," I replied. "I do it because inside of me it's something I know I'm good at. I can just feel it. It's something I was born to do."

Chapter 56

I respect every guy I get in the cage or ring with. Even though I believe I'll beat them, I understand that anything can happen in a fight. As I stood in the ring in the middle of a very quiet 13,000 people in the Yokohama Arena I was ready for, but respectful of Yoshiro Maeda.

When I say that the arena was quiet, I mean it. After we were announced we received polite clapping, and then it settled to the point that I could practically hear Michael Schiavello and Frank Trigg call the fight.

I believed that Maeda would come out fast and right at me. He did exactly that. As soon as the fight started he came forward while throwing punches from all angles. I landed a kick to the body. He caught me with a lead left hook. He stuck me with a stiff uppercut and I found myself against the ropes in the corner. I spun away and Maeda marched forward. I circled to my left.

Then Maeda reached for his eye and said something to the referee. The ref called time and I waited while the doctor looked at Maeda's eye. During the break, Frank Trigg talked about my game being on the ground and that I needed to go ahead and take Maeda down.

I'm sure he wasn't the only one thinking that, and the thought had crossed my mind as well, but once the fight restarted I landed some solid kicks.

Maeda rushed forward and threw a knee. I was in the corner again, but Maeda backed away.

I took the opportunity to push forward. We ended up sizing each other up in the center of the ring. We each threw a few feints and I noticed that his hands were low. He threw an uppercut that I saw coming, and then he landed a shot to my chest.

We exchanged again and I fired off an inside low kick to his right lead leg. As soon as I threw it he dropped his hands and leaned forward. His head was in perfect position and I shot off a left roundhouse that landed flush on the side of his face.

He fell backwards and I followed up by diving on him with a punch to make sure he was out. He was.

I jumped up and climbed the ropes to celebrate. In the U.S. the crowd would be going absolutely crazy. Here in Japan they stood and politely applauded. After climbing from the ropes I realized that Maeda was still down. I dropped to my knees and waited for the doctors to attend to him.

He was a warrior like me and he deserved the respect. Blood poured from his mouth and he stood on wobbly legs, but he appeared to be alright. I was given my trophy and stood for some photos, and then went to check on Maeda.

At the post-fight press conference they asked about my next opponent for Dream. They wanted to know who I wanted to fight. I told them that I did not ask for fights. Whoever they gave me I would fight, but first I would have to defend my belt back in the United States.

It had become apparent that Mikey McDonald was in line for another shot, and I guessed I'd be fighting him once again before I was able to return to Japan. I wasn't so fired up with the idea of fighting him. I'd beaten him handily the first time around and thought a rematch was too early.

I also guessed that a couple more wins would give me a great opportunity to make it into the UFC. Unfortunately, it wouldn't be so easy.

Chapter 57

Michael McDonald hit me again and again. He was all over me and I struggled to stay in the fight. I knew he'd be better than the last time we fought, but not this much better. Beforehand, I'd said that I expected the fight to go similarly to the first.

As Mikey took me down and roughed me up I was being blasted with the reality that the fight wasn't going anywhere close to the first one. My huge knockout of Maeda was a distant memory and as I struggled to keep from getting punched by Mike I saw my five-fight win streak fading away.

In round two I tried to regroup, but he beat me in every way. Without knowing what happened I was leaning against the cage and looking up at the referee, and then at Mike Popp. "Popp, give me my mouthpiece," I said.

"No, it's over, Cole."

"I'm fine. Give me my mouthpiece!"

"You got knocked out. It's over."

I had a hard time processing the words, but realized they were true. I'd lost for the first time since my return and my TPC belt was gone as well. After I recovered I congratulated Mikey. He deserved it. He'd improved a lot over the previous year and earned his revenge by knocking me out.

When I saw the video I knew how bad it was. I was basically out cold while leaning against the cage. I didn't fall down and took four or five hard shots while still on my feet. To this day it's tough for me to watch that one.

The first time around I was a big-name opponent for Mikey. Beating me would go a long ways in pushing his promising career forward. I spoiled the plans in that one, but this one was totally different.

I was somewhat numb afterward. I wondered what would have happened if I would have answered Sean Shelby differently. The WEC/UFC matchmaker had called me about three weeks before the McDonald fight. They needed a late replacement to fight Erik Koch.

My dream of making it to the UFC was a "yes" away, but I had to say no. I'd kept it to myself, but my rib got damaged during training. It kept popping in and out and I had to walk around with a body wrap just to keep it in place. It hurt like hell and there was just no way for me to take a huge fight on a few days' notice with such an injury. Plus I'd already signed on to fight Mikey again and I didn't want to back out. I wanted to keep my word even though I disagreed with the fight.

I understood that I could lose to Mikey, but everything had been going so well since my return. Now I was beyond frustrated because my chance at the UFC had passed, at least for now, and I'd suffered a bad loss.

I took a week or so off just to remind myself that there was more to life than fighting. I spent time with my family and tried to put everything into perspective. I hung out with Gabby as much as I could, and I'd been living with my new girlfriend.

She had a little boy that I was taking care of as if he was my own.

I constantly reminded myself that I had more than just fighting. Just the fact that I was walking around was a miracle. These thoughts made me appreciate life that much more.

My goal of getting into the UFC had taken a hit for sure, but it wasn't completely derailed. I got back in the gym and started training. I knew that if I started winning again and putting on exciting fights that my day would come, and then I got a call to replace Joe Warren at Dream 16 against Michihiro Omigawa. The fight was only ten days away and I knew almost nothing about Omigawa, but I took it in a heartbeat.

Chapter 58

I felt comfortable and relaxed being back in Japan despite being there without Mike Popp. He had already agreed to corner a teammate on the same day. I took my girlfriend along so she would get to experience Japan as well.

I knew Omigawa had high-level judo and despite having an 11-8-1 record he'd been in with some very tough guys. He'd fought in both Pride and UFC and had won seven of his last eight fights.

Still though, as I stood in the oddly quiet Nippon Gaisha Hall in Nagoya, Japan, I was calm and ready. We were introduced and then we met in the center of the ring for our brief instructions. We returned to the corner and the referee asked us if we were ready. We both nodded that we were. The bell rang and seemed to echo through the quiet arena. It was time to fight, and I was determined to get back on track.

Omigawa landed a couple punches and I delivered a knee before locking him up in a Muay Thai plum. We clinched and then went to the canvas. Omigawa was heavy as he sat in my half guard. I worked to get to full guard, but he managed to gain the mount.

I couldn't remember the last time I'd been mounted. I controlled his posture so he couldn't post up and beat the shit out of me. I wasn't afraid, more cautious. He landed a few good shots and I struggled to turn. Omigawa ended up in side control and that was an improvement for me. He looked for a guillotine choke, but I scrambled while looking for a reverse and ended up in his guard.

It was something of a relief to get to this position, but it didn't last. Omigawa started working on my left arm and I defended. I landed a few punches and then realized that he had my right arm locked up in a straight armbar. Before I could defend my elbow snapped.

The fight was over.

I stayed face down on the canvas with my arm hurting like hell. Shit, I'd lost two in a row after fighting so well for the last year and a half.

My arm throbbed as I pulled myself to my feet. Omigawa gave me a brief hug and I raised his arm in the air even as I grimaced in pain.

At the post-fight interview I sat with my right arm wrapped up in ice and tried my best to answer the reporters' questions. I told them that I was disappointed in myself and that I thought I had the advantage on the ground, but he beat me to the punch.

As the translator did her thing, I sat there and felt the anger boil inside. I was so fucking frustrated. Just six months earlier I'd been doing a similar post-fight interview in Japan after a huge victory. Back then the UFC was so close I could taste it, and then I even got the offer to fight. It was right there in front of me only months earlier. Now it was drifting over the horizon.

I guess it is the nature of the sport. The line between winning and losing can be so thin when there are so many paths to victory. Of course like all fighters I understood that concept, but as I sat there listening to the translator I felt the full brunt of it. I'd fallen to the wrong side of the line.

At the end of the interview I told them that I would be back. I really believed that, and yet I didn't know it at the time but I'd never fight in Japan again. It was back to the drawing board, and maybe a shot in the UFC was now far-fetched, but the thought of calling it quits didn't enter my mind.

Chapter 59

After returning from Japan I tried to relax and let my elbow recover. Again, I went back to spending time with family, but I kept my eyes on what was happening in the world of MMA.

The earlier rumors that the UFC would add the featherweight and bantamweight divisions were now seemingly very close to being reality. Towards the end of October of 2010, Dana White held a press conference and confirmed that they were adding the lighter divisions. During the conference he said, "This is a big day for the sport and the athletes who will have an opportunity to fight on the biggest stage in the world."

Those words rang in my head as I got back to training as hard as I could. I had to get another fight to begin to wipe away the last two losses. Then I started hearing other rumors that it was possible that The Ultimate Fighter season 14 could feature the new feather and bantamweight divisions.

I thought back to TUF 5 and how I was so close to getting on the show before the life-changing staph infection began to eat away my spine.

It was thought that the season would be sometime in the spring, so I knew I needed to get a fight, and a victory, before then. In January I got the call I was hoping for. Showdown Fights wanted me in Orem, Utah to take on a tough up-and-coming guy named Steven Siler.

On January 28th I found myself at Utah Valley University standing across the cage from Siler. We'd had a spirited run up to the fight. He was young and hungry and talked some smack beforehand. "I appreciate Cole stepping up to the plate and taking the fight, but it's probably a stupid decision because he's going down," Siler said in a pre-fight interview.

I kind of laughed off the comment, and later he said, "This is my shot. He's not going to take this away from me."

No doubt I could appreciate that sentiment, but what Siler didn't realize was that this fight was one of my last shots after ten years of scrapping and fighting and recovering and fighting some more. I absolutely had to have this win to keep the hope of reaching the UFC alive. I wasn't young anymore. It was now or never. And that was the difference between us. Despite having more fights than me, he would have many more shots after this fight. I wouldn't.

When taking the fight I'd talked with Mike Popp. "I've got to have this one," I said. "I don't know how much longer I can continue."

He nodded his head in understanding. "You'll get it. Do what you do best and stay focused."

That was exactly my plan. I didn't do anything special or train anything specifically for the fight. I knew what I could do and I planned on imposing my will on him and either knocking him out or submitting him.

Steven and I met in the middle of the cage for the main event. The crowd was fired up and loud, the exact opposite of Japan. We touched gloves and the referee told us to fight.

He tried to come out fast and we had a couple solid exchanges. He landed and I landed, and I ended up with my back against the fence. He took me down and tried to let loose with some ground and pound.

His punches were wild though, and in a matter of moments I had him locked up in my go-to sub, the triangle. He tried to stand to shake out of it, but I sank it in tighter. He dropped to his knees and I continued to apply pressure.

The ref was right on top of us and he immediately saw when Siler went out. He called off the fight and I rose to my feet.

I pretended to wipe the sweat off my brow and jumped on the cage to celebrate. I'd gotten back on track with the victory and now had a record of 17-6. I'd been in with some of the toughest guys in the world and had a real life comeback story to tell. If everything fell into place and TUF 14 ended up being for the lighter weight classes, I'd be there. I was sure of it.

Chapter 60

I was on the Underground MMA forum scrolling through threads and throwing in my two cents every now and then. The UG is a great MMA forum that has some of the biggest names in the industry posting on it. Even Dana White posts there from time to time.

A thread popped up about TUF 14, and it said that it was definite that it would be the lighter weights. I made a couple calls and found out that this was definitely the case. This was it. I'd get on TUF and tell my story to a national audience while showing my skills and personality.

I'd been told by the UFC higher-ups that after getting a belt I'd get my shot on the big stage. Unfortunately, after beating Jeff Bedard for the TPC belt I didn't get a call right away. It came a little later and I had to turn it down. I thought about that decision all the time. If I just would have taken the fight against Koch I would have reached my final dream of fighting in the UFC.

The Ultimate Fighter had been a launching pad for many careers. Its first season ended with a crazy slugfest between Forrest Griffin and Stephan Bonnar, and after that the show produced one UFC star after another. I set my sights on making my own splash during TUF 14. Of course first I had to get on the show.

The people at TUF sent me an application and I filled it out and returned it immediately. I then learned that there would be an open tryout in New Jersey in March. I tried to figure out how to get to it, but I just couldn't afford the flight and hotel. I thought this might hurt my chances a bit, but I was already known by the UFC. I'd been in contact with Reed Harris and Sean Shelby from time to time. And I had a pretty amazing comeback story.

It was around that time when I noticed a message on Facebook from a kid named Josh. I thought back and seemed to remember seeing his name on Twitter just a day or two before. I clicked on the message and gave it a quick read, and then I read it again.

The kid was in a wheelchair because of a staph infection. He wasn't asking for anything specifically, just looking for someone who could identify with his struggles and to tell me that I inspired him.

I sat back in my chair and stared at the screen for a long moment. His message really hit home. I was in a unique position to inspire others. A couple years ago, when I'd started my comeback, I'd talked about the importance of cleanliness and the overall awareness of the dangers of staph. Now after actually coming back I realized my role had shifted a little bit and I could actually inspire others to continue to hope.

I corresponded with Josh and then started hitting up people on the UG. I asked about getting him some weights and helping him out so he could keep his upper body in shape and keep fighting to walk again.

The correspondence with Josh made me that much more hungry to get into the UFC. It was a platform where I could really make a difference, and yet one day after another went by without a phone call.

I made an audition tape where I talked about my career and how this was real close to my last shot. It then showed my career highlights, and finished with me saving a cat that was stuck about thirty feet up in a tree.

It seemed like a great video, and I figured that there was no way TUF would pass me up. But I still didn't get a call.

Mikey McDonald had made it to the UFC. Michihiro Omigawa had mad it as well. And then we started hearing that guys were getting calls for TUF and Steven Siler was one of them. I'd just beaten him and yet he was getting a shot at TUF while I apparently wasn't. It seemed that all you had to do was fight me and you'd get in the UFC.

I decided that I needed to go on the offensive and sat down in front of the computer. I went to the UG and really became THAT guy. I was hateful and angry at the world. *This is bullshit...this is stupid...how could you be like this...* I started naming fighters either on the new TUF or in the UFC that I had already beaten or could beat. I just pretty much went crazy and I enlisted the UG for help with Twitter bombing Dana White. I tweeted to Dana about how I deserved the shot and I guaranteed that I would win if I could get on the show.

A bunch of UGers (Underground forum members) joined with me. Day after day we tweeted, sent Facebook messages, talked about it on MMA radio shows, anything I could do to finally make Dana think, *Fuck, I've got to shut this fucker up, just put him on the show!*

Our relentlessness increased and I began to hear rumblings that some of the UFC brass had taken notice. I wasn't sure if that was a good thing or not, and then my phone rang. It was Sean Shelby.

Chapter 61

I took a deep breath and then answered my phone. I really had no idea what to expect. Maybe he was about to tell me that all my bitching had landed me a spot on TUF. Or maybe he was about to tell me that Dana White was coming to my house with a baseball bat.

We quickly got the small talk out of the way, and then he said, "What are you doing? Why are you causing so much trouble?"

"You guys had a chance to pick me and you didn't. I tried out for TUF and you picked a guy that I just beat. I've tried every way that I could to get in. It just makes no sense."

I basically just laid it all out there for him and didn't pull any punches.

He tried to calm me down, but I was fired up. "Look, I'll fight Miguel Torres for free! I don't care. I want in and I'm ready to prove myself."

Sean said something along the lines of that being ridiculous and of course I'd be paid when I got my shot.

We talked for a while and he tried to explain that there was still hope for me to land a fight. I didn't see how that was possible, and told him as much.

Sean and I had had a solid relationship and I hated being this way toward him. I mean I knew that it wasn't like it was all his decision. At the moment he was just the guy on the other end of the line who got the brunt of my frustration.

"Well I'm sorry you feel that way," he finally said, "but you never know what can happen."

We hung up and I sat there seething. I felt like screaming because I was so damn close to reaching what was basically an unreachable dream, and yet they couldn't see that. They wouldn't open a door that I had been running towards for ten damn years!

I thought about our conversation and finally decided to call my mom. She had been with me every step of the way, and in a sense my dream of reaching the UFC was her dream as well. She hated seeing me fight, but she understood how much it meant to me.

"I got a call from Sean Shelby," I said.

"And?"

"And nothing, he wanted to know why I was causing so much trouble."

"What did you tell him?"

I told her pretty much what I had told him.

"Maybe there is a chance you'll get in but it won't be on TUF," she said.

"I doubt it."

"What are you going to do? Are you going to back off?"

"Fuck no," I said.

There was no real way to know what effect the online campaign was having on Dana or the other UFC brass, but I kept at it. It was now late April of 2011. It seemed that TUF was completely out of the question, and I was definitely not in the good graces of the UFC bosses.

The online campaign continued, but I needed a miracle to reach my dream. And then in early May I got another phone. It was Sean Shelby again.

Chapter 62

Once again, I had no idea what to expect from Sean. We'd kind of argued last time and he made it known that the UFC bosses didn't appreciate my campaign. However, I didn't stop after the call. In fact, the campaign had probably grown.

I breathed deeply and answered the phone. "What's up Sean?"

"Hey Cole, I've got a question for you." A handful of possibilities rushed through my mind. He continued. "Do you want to fight Renan Barão at 130 in a couple weeks?"

The words were coming out of my mouth before I even had a time to think. "Yeah, I'll take that fight."

Even though Sean and I had argued a bit, I could tell he was looking out for me. "Don't feel like you have to take the fight. He's a really tough opponent and it's on really short notice."

He was adamant about me understanding that this would not be my only shot.

I told him that I understood.

"You wanted in, and this is the only opportunity I have right now for you to be in."

"Yeah, I've talked to my coach about it and we both decided what the answer would be if I got the call."

"Well you wanted in, and this is in," Sean said. "You wanted your chance and this is definitely it."

We talked a while longer and he gave me some more specifics.

After hanging up the phone, I sat back and felt a wave of exhilaration wash over me. It had been ten long years and I'd endured being paralyzed. I'd won belts and I'd lost them and I'd been in against some of the toughest guys in the world.

I called Mike Popp and told him the news, and then I decided I would go see my mom in person. She had always been my number one supporter and now we'd reached this dream.

I got to her house and walked through the door.

"I've got some big news," I said.

"What is it?"

"Sean called. They want me to fight at UFC 130 in a couple weeks."

A look of excitement and spread across her face and she gave me a big hug. "I knew this day would come, Cole. You deserve it!"

I told her a little bit more and then decided it might be a good idea to get to the gym and start training for my UFC debut.

Chapter 63

The MGM Grand was absolutely crazy. I'd done my homework on Renan Barão and Mike and I thought that I had a good chance to beat him because I was an unknown to him and his camp.

I'd trained as hard as I could for the short time that we had, but now I walked around the MGM with a permanent smile plastered on my face. I'd finally made it to the UFC. I got in as much training during the week of the fight as I could, but I didn't even think much about Barão and his 25-fight winning streak. I could have been fighting Randy Couture and I still would have been smiling.

The fans were everywhere. They seemed to know where we would be even before we knew. I took photos with fans and joked with them. I even played a game of rock, paper, scissors with a guy for a signed UFC t-shirt.

I was tired and hungry as I worked to cut to the 135 pound limit, but I didn't care. Being at the MGM and in the UFC during the week leading up to the fight was so surreal. I felt like I was completely taken care of by the UFC. It is a marketing beast and they want the fighters to get out there and spend time with the fans and promote themselves.

We had a time-sensitive itinerary and were expected to be on time when they needed us somewhere. It is amazing how much of a well-oiled machine the UFC is. The first day I sat down in a room to sign posters. After I'd signed about five of them one of the staff members asked me if I was sure I wanted to keep signing them that way?

"Yeah," I said. "Why do you ask?"

He smiled. "Because you have to sign 150 of them during this sitting."

I started signing a little shorter and faster.

The UFC gave me all kinds of free stuff to give away to fans. I got literally a duffel bag full of swag to give out. I handed out shirts and photos and hats to fans as I laughed and joked with them.

We had an entire day set aside for media. I did one interview after another and spent time talking about what it was like to finally be here after such a long and difficult road. I spoke about how I felt that my fans, the people who had followed my career from early on or pulled for me during my comeback, were right with me. Since I had finally made it to the UFC it was as if they had made it here too.

Of course I also talked about the staph infection and paralysis and how there was always hope. I wanted to get as much of that out there because now I was on the biggest platform of my career.

Late on Thursday night I went down to check my weight. I walked into the back room the UFC uses as something like a mission control. Burt Watson and a few others were packing gear up and just shooting the shit. Burt is the UFC hype man and ensures everything runs smoothly. Joe Rogan calls him the babysitter to the stars. I don't think anybody could do his job as good as he does.

They were all just relaxing and listening to some great jazz music so I took the moment to just hang out and talk shop with them. Finally, I checked my weight and told them I needed to get some rest.

"You're a cool cat man. Here you go." Burt handed me a pair of UFC gloves.

"Thanks Burt," I said.

A year or so after this, my car was stolen and all of my UFC gear was inside except for that pair of gloves Burt gave me. They are my only memento of my time in the UFC.

That night I laid in bed in the darkness and stared up at the ceiling. Tomorrow I'd step on the scale and be face to face with Renan Barão.

I was ready.

Chapter 64

We were in a loosely formed line behind the curtain. I could hear the crowd on the other side. There had to be at least a couple thousand people waiting to watch the weigh in. Since I was the first to weigh in I stood just behind Joe Rogan, Dana White, Lorenzo Fertitta, Joe Silva, Marcus Luttrell the marine with the book Lone Survivor, and the Octagon girls.

It had been such a crazy week of meeting so many people that I'd seen on TV for so long. I'd talked with Dana White a couple times and he'd said he looked forward to my fight. I was here to fight, but in a weird way I was kind of a fan as well.

It was just surreal to be standing there behind the most powerful men in mixed martial arts after so many years of struggle and pain and doubt. It was overwhelming excitement mixed with a lingering sense that at any moment something would happen that would take this away from me.

The weigh in began and everybody in front of me filed out toward the stage as Joe Rogan announced them. I stood just on the other side of the curtain with Mike Popp and listened as the weigh in got underway.

"Let's get it started," Joe said. "In the bantamweight division Cole "The Apache Kid" Escovedo versus Renan Barão."

I was drained from the weight cut, but I felt a little jolt of energy hearing Joe Rogan yell my name. I walked up the stairs onto the stage and there was Burt Watson being his usual fired-up self. He told me to take off my stuff and get on the scale.

I did so and handed my clothes to Mike. I stepped up on the scale and looked out at the massive crowd. As Joe was reading my weight I held both hands up high and made the UG sign, thumb and pinky extended with middle finger up. The UG had been huge for me and I'd told them I'd send them some love.

After stepping off the scale I walked to my left and stood next to Dana White. Renan Barão was introduced and he stepped on the scale. There was talk that he was the next big thing. He'd won 25 fights in a row and many people thought he was on his way to the bantamweight belt. I had other plans for him. He weighed in at 135 as well, and then shook Dana's hand before raising his fists and stepping towards me.

I leaned in toward him and met his glare. I rocked back and forth while staring at him. The rest of the week had been exciting, but this was why I was here. Dana patted us each on the back and told us good luck. Barão and I shook hands and then I shook hands with Dana. As I left the stage I threw up the UG sign one more time.

Now it was all business. I was ready for this. I'd been ready for a long time. I knew Barão would be a tough fight, but I wouldn't have expected anything less from the UFC. It was time for the biggest fight of my career.

After the weigh in, I ate and rehydrated the best I could. Mike and I talked about our game plan and I saw the fight play out in my head. I was excited. Don't get me wrong, I was nervous as well, but I felt that my life had prepared me for this moment.

When I walked into the cage I'd be living out a dream that was supposedly impossible.

Chapter 65

I sat in the chair and tried to relax as Mike put the finishing touches on my hand wrap. The UFC actually has some of the best cutmen in the world to wrap your hands and the best, Stitch Duran, was scheduled to wrap mine, but I chose to have my coach do it. He'd done them from day one and this was the same job, just a different location.

The locker room was fairly quiet as a couple other guys on the card stretched and another relaxed on a bench waiting to get his hands wrapped. I breathed deeply and thought about my previous fights. I reminded myself that this was just another day at the office. It was just that the office was bigger.

Mike and I went through the game plan and I worked on the mitts and rolled on the mat that had been placed in the middle of the locker room. I built up a decent sweat and felt good.

Burt popped his head in the door. "You ready baby! This is it! Time to fight in the UFC baby! You go live in five. Remember to bring it!"

We walked out of the locker room door and down a hallway. Staff members pointed us in the right direction and we were stopped and told to wait. The music in the arena changed and a camera crew was in front of me.

A staff member told me to go.

I shook my hands out and started walking toward the Octagon. The hallway opened up into the MGM Grand Garden Arena and I felt a tingling sensation. The crowd cheered and I glanced up. My focus was solely on beating Renan Barão at that moment, but I also recognized how cool this was.

Later, after the fight when I had some time to reflect I realized that with each step toward the Octagon I was wiping away any past struggles and hardships, from my dad being sent to prison to my troubled high school years, to my few losses and any doubt they produced, right on through my staph infection and paralysis.

I was so excited as I reached the prep point to get my Vaseline applied. I was nervous, don't get me wrong, but I wasn't worried. This was where I was supposed to be even though I was told over and over that I would never make it.

I hugged my corner and the Vaseline was applied. I climbed the steps and touched the Mask sign that is permanently there to honor the late Charles Lewis, and then walked through the cage door to the Octagon. I circled and focused myself on fighting to the best of my ability.

The music changed and Renan Barão made his own long walk to the cage. Soon he was standing across from me. We eyed each other from across the cage and despite this fight happening in the UFC I knew that when the bell rang it would be just like my other fights. The two of us would do everything we could to beat the other.

Bruce Buffer appeared and started doing his thing. It was insane when he turned hard and pointed at me and yelled, "Cole "The Apache Kid" Escovedo!"

I'd imagined Bruce yelling my name to a crowd at least a thousand times over the last ten years. Now it was real.

Bruce introduced Renan Barão and I calmed myself and focused.

The smoker where I felt broken flashed through my head. The days in the casino where I drowned my sorrows flashed too. Then there was the beating of Mikey McDonald and the submitting of Steven Siler. I thought about my little girl and how I knew she was so proud of me, and how my mom, Laura, had done so much to help make this dream a reality.

Referee Steve Mazzagatti pointed at me and then at Barão. This was it. I was here. I'd made it against what were almost insurmountable odds. "Are you ready? Are you ready?"

We both nodded that we were, and then he told us to fight.

I walked to the center of the Octagon and touched gloves. I was exactly where I was supposed to be.

Epilogue

I ended up losing a tough decision to Renan Barão. I knocked him down in the second round and hurt him a bit. Barão went on to claim the bantamweight title and defended it multiple times before finally losing it to T.J. Dillashaw. Two of his opponents were guys I had fought, Mikey McDonald and Urijah Faber.

After the Barão fight I got a lot of props from the UFC. Sean Shelby told me not to take it the wrong way, they didn't bring me in to get hurt, but they thought Barão would be able to beat me handily. They were all impressed with how well I fought. My efforts in this fight scored me a match up on short notice with Takeya Mizugaki at UFC 135.

Mizugaki and I went after it in a great back and forth fight until he caught me late in the second and I lost by TKO. The fight was so good that it aired on the pay-per-view after the Jon Jones/Rampage Jackson main event.

After the fight we were told that it looked like we'd get the $75,000 bonus for fight of the night. I thought about what I could do with it. I could put money down on a house for me and Gabby or set up a college account for her.

It would have been a huge shot in the arm after suffering another loss, but Jones and Rampage put on a crazy fight and claimed the bonus. I still got a bonus because the UFC takes care of the guys who show up to fight, but it wasn't enough for a house.

I made more money while losing in the UFC than I had any the fights where I'd won with the exception of Japan. The UFC will take care of the guys who come to fight.

My last fight came just six weeks after the loss to Mizugaki. I was still recovering from that loss and had a messed up nasal passage, but I figured that since the UFC wanted me again I didn't want to say no. I had an uninspired fight against Alex Caceres and lost by decision.

I'd had enough. I'd reached an impossible dream by making it to the UFC after being told I would possibly never walk again. Now I was 30 years old and I'd put my body through it. After Caceres I went to Stanford to get reconstructive surgery and the doctor said it looked like I'd been kicked by a horse. There was no cartilage left and they needed to use a cadaver bone. I also had cartilage stuck in my nasal passage that made it almost impossible to breath.

The cumulative effects of a long fighting career coupled with the staph infection were taking their toll. I finally walked away from the sport and I was at peace with that. It was time to start a new chapter and follow my second love of dealing poker while spending time being a dad to Gabby.

When I look back over my life and my fighting career I am proud of what I have done. I've faced hardships and battled through them while living by that never quit mentality. I hope that my story can inspire others to do the same.

Thank you for taking the time to read my story. If you enjoyed it please tell others about it.